GOLF

THE ULTIMATE MIND GAME

GOLF

THE ULTIMATE MIND GAME

your path to *peak performance*

RICK SESSINGHAUS

Advantage™

Published by Advantage, Charleston, South Carolina.
Member of Advantage Media Group.

ADVANTAGE is a registered trademark and the Advantage colophon is a trademark of Advantage Media Group, Inc.

Printed in the United States of America

ISBN: 978-1-59932-030-4

Library of Congress Control Number: 2007921312

Most Advantage Media Group titles are available at special quantity discounts for bulk purchases for sales promotions, premiums, fundraising, and educational use. Special versions or book excerpts can also be created to fit specific needs.

For more information, please write: Special Markets, Advantage Media Group, P.O. Box 272, Charleston, SC 29402 or call 1.866.775.1696.

TABLE OF CONTENTS

acknowledgments

When I first started this book project I thought it would be simply me writing down all the knowledge that I had accumulated. I was wrong; the process of writing is difficult. This book could not have been completed without the help and support of many people. First off, a big thank you to all my past and current students who have always taught me about their own golf challenges. To my past teachers including Tom Barber, Paula Olsen, Ted Eleftheriou, and Brady Riggs, thank you for sharing your vast knowledge with me to make me a better player and teacher. To Dr. John Farley from the Optimal Performance Institute for teaching me the "real" performance skills. The long hours that Bill Kennedy helped me with structuring my ideas into words, I will be forever grateful. A special thanks to Yolanda Harris who has provided me with guidance in making my career successful.

My biggest thanks goes to my family which has supported me every "shot" along the way. My father, Rick who stepped up and became the one I bounced ideas off and who provided valuable insights. My mother, Sandy who continues to amaze me everyday with her strength and her constant support of my dreams. To my brother Steven who has taught me about never giving up. I am forever grateful to my beautiful wife Kathy and my three children Grace, Grant, and Katy who make all the hard work worthwhile.

Golf takes more mental energy, more concentration, more
determination than any other sport ever invented.
ARNOLD PALMER

So you want to play better golf and you are reading this book hoping it holds the secret. You may be frustrated that you are at the same handicap for the fifth year in row. Or are you the competitive type ready to pit your game against others. This book will help you shoot lower scores and provide you with the skills to play competitive golf with success. There is no secret to golf; however, there are mental skills that once mastered will make golf more enjoyable and lower your scores. The problem is these skills have been ignored by most golfers because they never truly understood what they were and how to improve them.

I also ignored this part of the game for many of my golf playing years. Once I figured out what really affects my scores, I decided to make a change and benefited from improved performance. In addition, I have shared these principles with my students who have reached new levels of performance. Whether I was working with a future U.S. Women's Amateur Champion or a beginner golfer who feared playing with his boss, I realized that my students needed more than just swing instruction. This book is not about how to grip the club or any other part of how to swing the club. This book is about the fundamentals of being your best, by being focused, emotionally ready, and pushing yourself to achieve more than you thought possible. While the game of golf is our primary subject, these principles may be applied to one's day-to-day life. Business performance, family dynamics, and other life roles all benefit from the lessons prescribed here. The mental game principles I learned not only saved my golf performance, it made it easier for me to deal with life's ups and downs. My journey from a beginner to a professional golfer started when I was twelve years old. A friend invited me to play at a local public course. I was instantly hooked by the challenge of a sport that seemed so easy at first glance. How hard could it be to hit a ball that was stationary? I found out quickly that golf was more than just chasing a little white ball around. That day changed my life; I was hooked!

As my obsession grew, I thought the quest for the perfect swing would make me a great player. As I bounced from teacher to teacher seeking the magic move, I ignored the other factors of performance. I slowly found that my attitude was getting worse and worse. I got angry on the course when the results of my shots were not what I expected. Then I got a wake-up call. One of my best friends and teacher told me after a round that she would not play with me again until I changed my attitude. I was a jerk on the course and was ruining the enjoyment for those who played with me. I ruined many family vacations because I would get depressed from playing poorly with my father. This attitude created a self-esteem problem—I was seeing myself as a failure. I not only had to change my golf game, but myself.

I changed my quest from a search for the perfect swing to learning what the best athletes did to achieve greatness. What I learned had very little to do with sport skills. The champions mastered mental and emotional skills to be the best. They blocked out distractions, had control over their emotions, and loved what they were doing. I went to school and studied Applied Sports Psychology and received my doctorate. I learned that it doesn't matter what sport a person plays, the mental skills are the same. I have loved helping athletes learn these skills and taking their game to the next level.

Teaching and playing golf for over twenty years has taught me that golf pushes you mentally and emotionally like no other sport. In fact it can make you feel a little crazy at times. The nicest people you meet in your daily encounters can become the angriest while on the golf course. Golf can bring out the worst in us. Golf is the ultimate mind game. You are alone matching your skills against the golf course. You have more time in between shots to think, which can be either positive or negative, depending on how you use it. Now is the time to learn the mental game skills so your performance improves and you get more enjoyment from the game.

As a golf professional it concerns me that so many people are not enjoying the game and many others have quit. The reasons are different for each individual, but we have lost sight of a simple truth: golf is a challenging game. That challenge makes golf a great game. To overcome the challenge a golfer needs to possess not only golf skills, but must be mentally tough. The problem is most people believe golf should be easy. It is not. This belief leads to frustration and self confidence problems.

How can we start playing golf at a better level and start enjoying it more? Golf requires many factors to play at one's best. These include learning the mechanics and skills of the game which will improve with professional instruction. With all the changes in equipment it is a must to have properly fit equipment, which will make you more consistent. Golf's other factor that is finally getting the attention it deserves is the physical fitness of the golfer. I have a great relationship with the leaders in golf fitness, Body Balance for Performance, and currently work with fitness experts Keith Kottering and Eric Fleishman with www.Ericthetrainergolf.com. One's physical conditioning can help or hinder performance and we all need to address this part of the game. This last factor is my passion; the mental and emotional aspects of the game. Golfers need to develop these skills to maximize their performance. I have taught traditional golf instruction and it works to a point. There are many players out there who have tremendous amounts of knowledge but they don't know how to apply it on the course and most importantly don't enjoy the process.

I am a big believer that the more you enjoy doing something the better you will get at it. This is especially true with golf. Too many people spend hours playing and practicing a game that usually creates more frustration than joy. The mental game of golf is finally getting the recognition it deserves. With elite players seeking help from sports psychologists, acceptance from the average golfer is also growing.

When I ask students if the mental game is important, I first get a blank stare and then I get a, "sure it is important." I then ask them what the mental game is and I again get a blank stare. Getting golfers to admit that they need help with the mental side of golf is a problem. They don't know what constitutes the mental game and have no idea how they might work on these skills. I have written this book for three reasons: (1) to clarify what the mental game of golf really is; (2) to provide you with the necessary mental skills for peak performance; and (3) to give you a plan to implement in order to learn and master these skills.

The definition of golf's mental game that I will be using is, one in which you the golfer is fully integrated with all of the mental performance factors. Those factors include motivation, focused attention, emotional stability, physical state management, and committed execution. In other words, you will have a goal to learn how and what to concentrate on, how to acquire a winning attitude, and how to be in control of how you are on the course. All of these lead to golf execution at the highest level. These factors can all be learned. In fact, you have done each one well in the past whether you know it or not.

What makes up the game of golf? To be the best golfer you can be requires you to master all the performance factors of golf. Developing actual golf skills is the first factor. This consists of learning a consistent, repeatable swing that maximizes distance with proper direction. A golfer must also learn many different short game skills such as putting, chipping, pitching, and bunker play. The list of all the shots you will play in your golf career is lengthy. You must learn the mechanics of these shots to give yourself the best chance to execute them. Learning the proper mechanics requires professional instruction and proper practice.

Good golf requires a certain amount of physical conditioning. Maximum performance requires flexibility, strength, balance, posture, and core conditioning to play your best golf, injury free. Caring for your body means eating right and providing your body with plenty of water to stay hydrated. Consult a professional trainer or seek out the fitness experts at www.Ericthetrainergolf.com for further details on conditioning and nutrition. Working with a trainer and doing even a small amount of exercise can benefit you immensely.

The tools of the trade can affect your golf performance. Your golf equipment is another factor that can make a big difference in your consistency. Now it is easy to be fitted like the professionals. Take the time to make sure you have properly fit equipment. With the advent of launch monitors you can gain twenty yards by just switching a driver and golf ball. By seeing a professional club fitter you will gain confidence in your equipment and get the most out of your golfing mechanics.

This book is about the mental and emotional factors of golf. Golf is a unique game; the ball doesn't move and there is a lot of time between shots. These factors challenge the golfer to stay focused, be mentally tough, and execute despite fears and doubts. Here's where I can help you. I understand the mental factors of golf and I realize that the ability to take your game to the next level has more to do with your mental and emotional skills than what ball you play. Every sport requires the ability to be mentally sharp and emotionally strong. Now is the time for you to be that golfer. The psychology of golf is still a misunderstood factor. Golfers are confused by what it is and how to improve it.

Let's examine some myths about golf psychology:

- The only golfers that need mental training are head cases. Normal golfers don't need golf psychology

  o The truth is all golfers can benefit in some way from golf psychology. Different topics that can be covered include: clarifying goals, improving concentration, improve emotional stability, learning to relax. Every golfer can improve all aspects of his mental games.

- Mental training is only a band-aid to help golfers out of a slump

  o Proper mental training is helpful as a way to prevent golfers from poor performances. Mental training, used consistently will help build confidence now and in the future.

- Sport psychology coaches cannot relate to golfers

- Most sport psychology coaches have played sports at some level and that experience has fostered their educational pursuits. Mental skills are similar with all sports.

- Golf psychology is basically pop psychology

  o Golf psychology is based on the field of sports psychology which has been researching what works with elite athletes. These techniques have been proven to work.

- Working with a sports psychology coach is only about finding what's wrong with a golfer.

  o No, it is more about reminding the golfer what they already know how to do. Learning from your past successes can be a lot more beneficial than rehashing your current failures.

- Golfers believe they don't have time to train mentally

  o Most mental training requires no special equipment, just a quiet place to practice techniques. The techniques can be done in as few as five minutes. Mental training requires you to make shifts in how you think. Awareness of your thinking is the first step in mental training. Once you become aware of how you are thinking you can began to see if your thoughts are helping or hindering your golf performance.

My premise is this: your thoughts create your level of success. I will be sharing the latest performance psychology skills to improve how you think to achieve a new level of success. An equation that I will be referencing throughout the book is:

Your <u>Thoughts</u> lead to <u>Beliefs</u> which leads to <u>Emotions</u> which leads to <u>Attitude</u> which leads to your <u>State</u> which leads to your <u>Behavior</u> that creates a <u>Result</u> = **Level of Success**

We are going to explore how we can change the detrimental parts of this equation so you will develop a new level of performance on and off the course. For example if you have beliefs that you are a poor putter it will create a different result then if you have a positive belief about your putting. You are different from every other golfer. You react to what happens on the golf course in different ways. Some people throw clubs after a poor shot; others laugh off a poor shot. You experience life and golf differently than anybody else. Are you reacting to your golf game in positive ways that help performance or in negative ways that detracts from performance?

To be the best you can be takes work. Taking action toward your golfing goals should be fun, but it requires commitment. Even though all golfers are looking for the magic cure that will solve everything, we all know deep down that golf requires consistent practice and a positive attitude to deal with the ups and downs of the game. This book is not about being average, which is easy. This book is about reaching your potential and enjoying the journey. Many have tried and have failed to improve their golf game by just working on their golf swing mechanics and still find themselves shooting the same score. It is time to work on your entire game which includes the mental game. If you master the tools and techniques in this book, you will lower your scores, while enjoying the game more than ever.

Learning the mental skills is a process. Similar to like when you learned to swing a club; we all go through different levels to attain and master them. When you learn these new mental skills you will also go through these levels to mastery.

Practice puts your brains in your muscles.
SAM SNEAD

The five levels of skills development are:

- Level 1- Unconscious Incompetence- We don't know how bad we are

- Level 2- Conscious Incompetence- Know that we don't possess the necessary skills to meet the challenge. We need to think about our mechanics and practice to develop new skills. The mind works over-time to learn new skills. We know we are beginners and constantly are processing all of the information that will help us become competent. This is a time of information overload. The mind is used to process new information, which makes it more difficult to execute the skill proficiently.

- Level 3- Conscious Competency- With practice we have developed the skill. We can give ourselves less instruction and develop some confidence. We have learned the basics and can execute a variety of shots. We have practiced enough to know we can do it, but not enough to not think about how to do it.

- Level 4- Unconscious Competency- We possess a high degree of confidence in our mechanics and our muscle memory takes over. At this stage the swing thoughts are minimal and new instruction is minimal. We can play with minimal interference.

- Levels 5- Unconscious Mastery- We have developed confidence in all areas of our skills. There are no mechanical thoughts. Our body is controlled by our unconscious. This is the zone.

Let's get ready to enter your golfing zone!

YOUR SHOT

- What has your golf journey been and where do you want it to go?

- What level are your golf skills?

- Are you open to learning the mental skills of golf?

chapter

(1)

WHAT IS THE MENTAL GAME?

WHAT YOU WILL LEARN:

• The Evolution Of Golf's Mental Game

• The Nine Principles Of The Mental Game

• Measuring Where You Are Now

*Golf's a compromise between what your ego wants you to do,
what experience tells you to do, and what your nerves let you do.*
BRUCE CRAMPTOM

The person I fear most in the last two rounds is myself.
TOM WATSON

The first question I am asked as a Sports Psychology Coach is, "what is the mental game anyway?" The mental game is a vague term that means different things to different people. Some might think that a golf/sport psychology coach would have you lie on a couch and share your deep down problems stemming from your childhood. I view the field of golf's mental game as a way to improve an individual's performance based on psychological performance issues. This is the here and now of someone's performance. I rarely talk with golfers about their childhood experiences. I want to know what you want, why you haven't got it, and ways to bring your goals into reality.

Sometimes it is something simple that can be handled in a few minutes, while other times it may require some consistent work. I believe as a performance coach I am there to remind you of something that may be simply forgotten. I ask pertinent questions, make some suggestions, and teach some tools and techniques in order to play to a higher level.

Golfers for years have known how important the mental game is to playing well. Bobby Jones was talking about the mental game with his famous quote, "The most important part of golf is the six inches between the ears." The late 1980s saw a shift in the acceptance of players working on the mind game to improve performance. Players such as Nick Price, Davis Love III, and Tom Kite started working with prominent sports psychologists and expressed how this helped their game. In last twenty years more players at every level are reading books on the mental game and seeking out coaching sessions.

There has not been a lot of research in the field of golf psychology showing proof of how certain techniques affect performance. But in the last five years research studies have increased and the results can help us all to improve our performance. In this book I have combined my experience as a professional golfer, a current performance coach, and the research from leading experts in the field of sports psychology, to educate you to tap into the benefits of training the mind. Training the mind will keep you focused no matter the pressure to allow you to execute your best swing, and to help you enjoy the game more.

What does the mental game of golf mean to you? Common answers I have received are: confidence, focus, dealing with pressure, and attitude. My definition of the mental game includes these aspects: golf is a mind/body activity, the mind and body work together to create action. The goal is to master the mind skills to help the body work more effectively. I want golfers to move closer to playing in the zone. The zone is a buzz word that describes a time of peak performance. Many studies have been completed on the state of zone.

The zone experience is made up of these sensations:

- No conscious thinking of how to perform

- Total immersion in activity

- Narrow focus of attention

- Feeling of being in control

- Effortlessness

As golfers, we are always looking to get better. Part of the process is understanding what skills you need to develop to get to the next level. Start identifying which of your mental skills need to be improved. Below are the skills that you will need to master to achieve peak performance for your golf game.

1. Motivation- stay excited about playing golf

2. Goal Setting- know what you want

3. Beliefs- be confident in your ability

4. Emotional Stability- staying mentally tough

5. Planning- knowing how you will improve

6. Focus- blocking out distractions

7. Execution- making a committed swing

8. Evaluation- learning from your results

9. Enjoyment- having fun

At the beginning of any important project we must know where we are before we can move forward. Here are some questions about your mental game of golf. Answer them honestly so you can see where improvement is needed to reach your best.

Do you look forward to practicing? Yes

Do you know what you want to accomplish with your golf game? sort of!

Have you experienced self doubt about pulling shots off? yes

Do you play your best golf or your worst golf when you feel pressure? worst

Can you stay focused on hitting your shots for the entire round of golf? most of the time, unless I make repeated terrible shots

Do you find yourself getting frustrated on the course? Sometimes

Are you making the same mistakes on the course that you did last year? fewer, but some; far fewer strategy mistakes

Do you have fun playing golf? Yes

Now that you know where you are, you can begin to fill in the gaps of your skills. Filling these gaps in performance will take your game to the next level. Awareness is the first step to optimal performance. The next step is to implement the new skills and then mastering them. Let's learn the first skill, motivation.

YOUR SHOT

- How do you define the mental game?

- What are the three areas of your mental game that need the most improvement?

chapter

(2)

MOTIVATION

WHAT YOU WILL LEARN:

- Understanding your reason for playing

- What affects motivation

- The different types of motivation

- How to stay motivated

*I'm sick of playing lousy... First it irritates you, then it really bothers you,
until finally you get so damn blasted mad at yourself that you decide
to do something about it. I've decided to do something. And I will.*
JACK NICKLAUS

*At some point, you say to yourself, 'I want to be the best.'
But when you honestly make the commitment,
you have to realize all the dedication and time that it takes.*
RAYMOND FLOYD

chapter

2

When I ask my clients what do you want to accomplish in golf, I often get a blank stare or the general answer, "I want to play better." We need to know what we want specifically before we know how to get there. When we turn our attention to what we want we become more focused, motivated, and use our time more wisely. Golfers who make the biggest improvements know specifically where they want to go and in what time they want to get there. Components of motivation involve having a dream, a vision on how to accomplish the dream, the desire to keep working despite the obstacles, and loving what you do. Motivation is the drive that leads to action being taken toward a desired goal.

The fundamental idea of traditional motivation revolved around what you want to accomplish. A more important question would be why do you play golf? Reread that question. Why do you play golf? This question confuses many because they may not know the reasons. Seems like it would be obvious, but sometimes our reasons for playing have changed without us knowing. The answer to this question sets the stage for what motivates you to play. Do you play for the challenge, the time with family, the social aspect, the recreation, the competition, for business, or another reason? I want you to know why you play. If you have an exciting enough reason to play you will be motivated to improve your performance. Change the way you describe golf by using words that create more positive emotions. An example would be instead of, "I play golf because of the challenge," replace it with, "I enjoy playing golf to feel the challenge to push myself to higher levels." The emotional "why" statement should make you passionate to play. Becoming passionate adds to the motivation and helps you when your game is down. Remind yourself everyday why you play or practice and why you are investing your time in golf. Be passionate!

Your reasons for playing can change as you continue to play. Some start playing for the exercise and as they get hooked, they begin to play for the competition. The reason you play will affect what you want out of golf. An average tour professional plays golf purely as a career to make a living, while Tiger Woods plays golf to rewrite history. Tiger has stated his intention to break Jack Nicklaus' major victory total of eighteen professional majors. This goal has produced a tremendous drive in Tiger to be the best of all time. His work ethic is the best. He dedicates his time to physical and mental training, and practice time. He does whatever it takes to reach his goal. His reason for playing is to challenge himself to be the greatest ever. His actions need to match that goal. So I ask you again, why are you playing golf?

Use these empowering questions to reconnect to your reasons for playing golf:

1. What is fun about golf?

2. What do you love about golf?

3. Why did you first play golf?

TYPES OF MOTIVATION

INTRINSIC/EXTRINSIC

There are different ways to motivate your golf game. The ways we look at the game are very important. Two types of motivation, intrinsic and extrinsic can be very powerful, yet one can produce some negative consequences. What motivates you to play? This is different then why you play. I want to know if you are motivated by internal reasons (intrinsic) or if you need outside influences (extrinsic) to get you hyped to play. Some people are motivated by just playing a round of golf by themselves while others only get motivated if there is something on the line. This happens to tournament golfers who see golf as purely a competition against others; the bigger the tournament, the bigger the motivation.

For many of my competitive clients, motivation is only focused on the next tournament. The cycle becomes, as tournament season comes closer than practice increases; when no tournaments are scheduled, the practice decreases. If competition is the only motivation then you will not have a consistent work ethic, and if performance in those tournaments is poor than motivation will suffer. Create goals that are not just about playing in tournaments. Create intrinsic goals like enjoyment, personal challenge, and social aspects to balance out the competitive drive.

Do you play for the internal satisfaction that golf provides? Do you practice for the sheer joy of hitting balls or does there have to be a reason to practice? Will you only practice because there is an important tournament coming up or a grudge match with your weekend foursome? Do you need external rewards to get you to play? Why do you play? This question asks a lot about your game as well as what the level of your game will be in the future.

PAIN/PLEASURE

Another aspect that motivates people to take action revolves around the pain/pleasure principle. People do things to gain pleasure or avoid pain. Are you motivated to practice and play because you gain pleasure from the idea of playing for success? Or are you motivated by the fear of failure? Most golfers are motivated by the pain principle. I used to have clients who took instruction because they were going to play in a business golf tournament and did not want to embarrass themselves. These golfers are motivated by pain. They will cram practice time in at the last possible moment to avoid potential embarrassment. After the tournament is over the golfer stops practicing because the threat of pain is no longer there, until, of course, the next business tournament rolls around. This type of motivation works short term, but creates the potential for burnout if it becomes the only reason for taking action.

A preferred motivation is to take action that gives pleasure. Using the above example, the golfer would take lessons and practice to experience playing well. The golfer could also want to play to enjoy the company of co-workers. Many of my students look forward to playing with their spouses on vacations. Golf becomes something that the couple can share and the score becomes secondary. When you look forward to playing to experience joy, your motivation will be consistent throughout the year. This attitude will motivate the golfer to play golf without worrying about negative consequences of embarrassment. Are you motivated to practice and play golf to avoid pain or experience pleasure? If it is about pain, now is the time to rethink your reasons for playing.

Practice to build skill, not to avoid embarrassment

MOVING AWAY/MOVING TOWARD

Similar to the pain/pleasure principle is the moving away vs. moving toward motivation. This is when a golfer is motivated to practice and play to move away from something rather than toward something. Moving away would be, "I practice golf, so I won't be terrible." Moving toward would be, "I practice golf so I can become a better golfer." The level of golf may be the same; however, how you view it will certainly affect your motivation. Begin to shift any reasons that are away reasons and make them toward reasons. Statements such as, "I can't wait to learn a new shot," and "I am looking forward to the challenge of playing with better players," are empowering statements. They will motivate you by changing your focus to positive aspects, instead of focusing on what you don't want. Moving toward is more powerful in the long run than moving away.

VALUES

The last area of what motivates you is a combination of some of the previous aspects of motivation. It is your values. Values are what are important to you. If it is important for you to play for social reasons, you will not be motivated to play by yourself. If it is important that golf be a way to release stress you will not put yourself in a competitive situation that increases stress. The way to connect with your values is to ask, "What is important to me about playing golf?" Once you have the answer you can organize your rounds around those reasons. You will enjoy yourself more and play better golf. I have seen when people compromise their reasons to play and it has been detrimental. I have had students who loved going out to play for recreation and then start gambling with playing partners and it shifts the outcome from fun to worrying about competing. This happens with junior golfers all the time. They want to play golf for fun and their parents want them to play in tournaments. The juniors end up playing in tournaments and not enjoying playing the game. Play for your reasons, not someone else's.

There are times when your motivation to practice or play might not be there. If you do play, you are not fully engaged in each shot. When you just go through the motions this is a motivation problem, which includes burnout, lack of practice, and lack of enjoyment. I have seen this happen with every level of golfer. What effects a player's motivation could be poor performance, changing of reasons to play, or not meeting expectations. Everyone's game has its ups and downs, yet the best are still motivated to practice to get better. When our performance does not match our expectation we become frustrated. The best players use frustration to create motivation to get better, while others let frustration stop them from taking action. When you stop taking action, you are no longer motivated.

To develop motivation you can do three things: (1) Reconnect to a powerful reason to play, (2) Create exciting goals that will spur you on, (3) Get instruction to help you through a period of down performance. I experienced a low in motivation when my performance suddenly deteriorated. I went from shooting under par to not being able to break 80. I didn't enjoy playing and practicing made me even more frustrated. My attitude was getting so poor that I didn't even want to watch golf on television.

I took a few months away from the game to reevaluate why I was playing. That time away gave me a fresh outlook on how lucky I was to be able to play the great game of golf. I remembered why I loved golf and I began to honestly look at what I needed to do to both play better and more importantly enjoy the game. I decided to play more with friends and compete less. I went back to my old instructor and practiced the simple things that had made me a good player. I was now playing for my own reasons and allowed myself to not have to shoot par to enjoy the game. When motivation is lacking, take the time to reevaluate what you want from the game and what you are willing to do to achieve it.

I have found the following to be a very destructive statement that some players have expressed to me. "If I do all this hard work and I don't achieve my goal, then I wasted all that time." This is not spoken by someone who is an intrinsically motivated golfer. So I then pose the question, "Would it be better to give less than 100% effort and not reach your goals regretting that you didn't do everything you know you could have done to achieve a higher level?" The answer is obvious. As humans we like to have a scapegoat. We fear that our best is not good enough so why go all out to experience that disappointment? Personally, I was a lot more proud of myself for giving it my all and coming up short than the times I gave it less than my best. Take pride in yourself and let whatever outcome happen. Embrace the journey toward your goal and you will learn a lot about yourself.

Even though I want golfers to be motivated no matter the obstacle it is important to have a support system when even your motivation can't get you out of negative thinking. This is where a friend or coach can help pick you up when performance is suffering. Part of my job as a sports psychology coach is to support and create ways to rekindle the drive of an athlete when the challenges seem too great. In golf your goal may not be to win the U.S. Open; however, when you have a poor round it is nice to be able to vent some of the frustration. Your playing partners probably don't want to hear it, so find someone who will just listen. They don't have to give advice. Most time by talking it out you will be able to bounce back and look forward to the next time you play.

When I have been in a motivational rut, I go back to when I enjoyed golf the most. My fondest memories of golf were when I was a teenager and played by myself. I would close up the golf shop I worked at and played until it got dark. I would play two balls and pretend I was playing against either Fred Couples or Nick Faldo. I remember how peaceful an experience it was and would race around to squeeze in another hole even though I couldn't see my ball. To me that was more enjoyable than winning a club championship or playing in a professional tournament. It was just me and the course. I could try new shots, not caring about the result. I let my imagination control what shot I would hit next. I played free of pressure and loved every minute of it. That was almost twenty years ago. Now I will go out and play a quick nine holes in the morning to reconnect with my strongest reason to play.

If we play golf long enough our reasons for playing will change. I refer to this as your relationship with golf. My twenty years plus of golf have been a love/hate relationship. What started out as just a game, became a career, then it went back to just a game, and now golf encompasses business reasons and personal reasons for why I play. If you learned golf as a child it was probably for the true love of the game. Maybe it was something you could share with your father, mother, or friends. Now as you grew older golf can mean something different. When you identify your reasons for playing, you help to maintain your motivation to keep playing.

YOUR SHOT

- What is your powerful "why" for playing golf?

- Are you playing for internal satisfaction or external rewards?

- What needs to change for you to improve your motivation?

- Commit to play for your own reasons.

chapter

GOAL SETTING

WHAT YOU WILL LEARN:

- How To Identify What You Want

- How Goals Provide Motivation

- Clarify How You Are Going To Accomplish
  Your Goals

A champion must have the will to win not just the wish to win.
You have to have an attitude that says,
"I know I can do it! And I'm going to do it!
PATTY BERG

My only goal is to look back at the end of each year
and see that I have improved.
JIM FURYK

chapter

(3)

To improve at any endeavor requires knowing what you want and how you are going to get it. Being motivated is the first step in getting to the next level with your game. When you are excited, the work involved to get better is a lot easier. Motivation is the fuel on the fire that propels you to take on your goals. However, you need to have goals for that motivation to be useful. After this chapter you will identify what you want to accomplish with your goals and what is required to accomplish them.

Goal setting is a process that defines what you want to accomplish. Goal setting has been a fundamental technique used for decades by world-class athletes to bring their performances up to the next level.

Goal setting provides:

1. Excitement

2. A plan

3. Clarity

4. Motivation to take action

Goal setting has been a popular technique to achieve success for quite some time. However, proving that goal setting works has been difficult. Many successful individuals have shared their secrets of success and it usually includes goal setting. With performance psychology there are many ways to create goals. My method brings together the best of the best. This method of creating outcome, performance, and process goals has been popularized by champion athletes. You can now use it for your golf game.

Research has validated that each part of the goal-setting program is important. Having outcome goals creates motivation. Knowing performance goals creates stepping stones to provide the athlete with direction. Yet the most important goal from a performance standpoint is the process goal. A research study completed at the University of Northumbria at Newcastle, UK, showed that when athletes had process goals for before and during performance their concentration skills improved. The study goes on to say that process goals can be combined effectively with the motivational benefits of performance and outcome goals. What this study shows and what great golfers know already is that you must place your attention on the process of your performance. Give up the winning and losing and create goals that make you perform "in the now." This is why pre-shot routines are taught by so many sports psychology coaches. The routine is a technique to get you in the now. Having a pre-shot routine would be part of a process goal. The process goal might be 100% commitment to every shot. Each shot has a goal that is under your control. The problem is that golfers stay in the outcome goal of "I want to hit this shot in the middle of the fairway." That is a great intention; however it is not totally in your control. You could hit the ball as you intended, yet hit a sprinkler head and bounce in the water. Have the outcome goal become your target and have your process goal be what you can do to make it happen. Commitment to shot or staying focused on staying present would be the process goal to include in your game.

When goal setting is brought up most people think of outcome goals. These are goals with a very specific result. An example would be becoming a single digit handicap golfer. A lot of golfers have these types of goals at the start of the golf season. This is the basic level in goal setting. What do you want to accomplish? I encourage my students to create outcome goals at the start of the year. As the coach I now have a better understanding of what students want and how I might be able to help them to attain these goals. Also, the goals help gauge their commitment level. As a coach I can help sustain motivation even when their game is "not up to par." Outcome goals need to be created with specific steps.

The goals need to be:

1. Specific/Measurable – how will we know when you accomplished it

2. Time sensitive – when will you accomplish this goal

3. Challenging – outside your current comfort zone

4. Exciting – makes you want to practice

Creating goals that are measurable is a very powerful tool. When a goal is measurable it becomes something your mind can grasp. Goals are concrete and you will know when you have reached them. Having goals that can't be measured lead to confusion, laziness, and lack of focus. Unfortunately most golfers either don't create goals and vague goals don't provide the benefits of setting correct goals. Having a goal helps provide the motivation and sets the standard for your desired performance.

Many golfers are afraid to set goals because they will feel like a failure if they don't reach them. This is a cop out. These people never take the necessary risks to push themselves to higher achievement. Some use goals to make themselves feel better by choosing goals that are too easy to accomplish. Goal setting should be used to help you raise your standard of performance. Weak goals produce weak results. Go for those goals you were afraid to admit. Maybe you are an 18 handicap golfer who wants to be a 9 or a 9 wanting to be a scratch. I applaud your vision for becoming something more than you are now.

The next step for making goals a reality is creating a time frame in which you will accomplish the measurable goal. I encourage you to write out long-term goals (Ultimate goal, 3 years or more), middle range (1-3 years), and short term goals (under a year). Short term goals will be the most important tools to help you along your road.

Treat the goal setting process as a journey to a destination. Along the way you are going to arrive at several destinations before you reach your ultimate point. Many sports psychology coaches have their athletes focus on the ultimate goal as their driving force. The problem with this is that if the ultimate goal is too far into the future the golfer becomes frustrated because there is no way to measure if you are on the right path to accomplishment. An ultimate goal is the first place to start. However, you need to break down this goal into more short-term goals. By working backwards from your ultimate goal you can trace all the way to what needs to be accomplished today. A golfer now is clear on the path and clear on the activities that are necessary to move forward. This boosts confidence in the golfer because a measurable plan of action with motivating goals has been formulated.

Start with your long-term vision. What do you want to accomplish? What is your ultimate goal? As a junior golfer it might be to play on the PGA/LPGA tour. These goals might be far off, yet they are great to start the goal setting process. We use long-term goals to develop a plan. You can then move backwards on a time line. This process is called chunking down. Take your ultimate goal and break it down into smaller bite size pieces. This exercise is your future time line of your golf career.

This is how it works we take our ultimate goal and place it at end of the time line.

-- *Win Major Championship*

Notice I put a very high goal in that spot. For this exercise I want to show you how we can chunk it down. The next spot I need to chart is your current level. You need to be honest with yourself. For this example the golfer is a junior golfer who's a five handicap golfer. A five handicap golfer is a very good golfer; however, not yet close to an elite, major winning professional.

[--]
5 handicap golfer   *Major winner*

This process of chunking down your goals is very important because, if our only goal was winning a major championship, we could easily be frustrated and disillusioned. We would be so far away from accomplishing it, that the motivation would tend to be minimized. The reason we have goals is to know what we want; it creates motivation. The goal with the time line exercise is to know what needs to happen now in order to work closer toward the goals. Filling in the time line creates realistic goals along the way to your ultimate goal. The rest of the time line exercise is to fill in the measurable goals that will lead to the highest outcome goal. These are progressively more difficult accomplishments in the order that they would happen. I have filled in the rest of the timeline. Notice that there are many steps along the timeline.

Current Level- five handicap

Next level- Scratch handicap

Next level- College player

Next level- Top Amateur

Next level- Winner on Professional Mini-tour event

Next level- Qualify for PGA Tour

Next level- Contend in a PGA Tour event

Next level- Win a PGA Tour event

Next Level- Contend in a Major Championship

Last Level- Win a Major Championship

Someone could win a major without accomplishing the other steps, but it is unlikely. I have seen the trend toward young players skipping years of college to turn professional. There are only a few who have accomplished the previous steps to be ready for the next level of professional golf. Even top amateurs have found the transition to the next level more challenging than they thought it would be. It is easy to get ahead of ourselves and think we are ready for the next level.

I was working with a client who was a fifteen handicap who wanted to be a nine handicap in eight months. That is a challenging outcome goal which required a plan for improvement. He also wanted to play in tournaments for the first time. He experienced tournament golf while playing in the monthly men's club and city championships. These two outcome goals created motivation in him to work hard. He assessed where his game was and prioritized what needed the most work. He changed his practice habits, by working on becoming a straighter driver and converting more up and downs around the green. To play in tournaments he started with small club tournaments before he played in the state net championship. This progression from smaller tournaments to bigger tournaments helped him mentally get accustomed to the different tournament pressure. After each tournament we would evaluate his performance and make adjustments in his process goals to keep him on track toward his outcome goals. In that eight month period he won two club tournaments and was in contention for the state net championship. At the end of the golf season his handicap was a nine. He then came to me and identified his next set of goals which was to get down to a four handicap in the next twelve months. His understanding of setting outcome goals and forming performance goals made it easy for him to see what needed to be improved. What he did better than those who just have outcome goals was his commitment to the consistent process goals of his practice sessions. He stayed focused on accomplishing the weekly process goals which lead to accomplishing his outcome goals.

Right now I want you to map out your outcome goal steps to your ultimate goal. Now that we have identified what your outcome goals will be, it is time to fill in the rest of the goal setting process. Below is the entire process of goal setting which will give you a plan to move ahead and finally reach your golf goals.

The process of goal setting:

1. Starts with a <u>Dream</u>- the ultimate you want to accomplish with your golf game. A dream doesn't provide you with the how.

2. <u>Outcome goals</u> are those measurable milestones that are exciting to pursue. These can be big or small, long-term or short-term. When I was in high school my long-term goal was to play collegiate golf. My short-term goal was to average 76 for my high school matches. It is important to balance out outcome goals to include both short-term and long-term. Having both will provide consistent motivation to keep working on your game.

3. <u>Performance goals</u>- the standard of performance required to accomplish the outcome goals. The best way to identify a performance gap is to ask good questions. For example: what is preventing you from achieving your goal? It could be swing mechanics, or physical conditioning, or confidence. When you identify the reasons for why you haven't achieved your goals, you have taken the first step in doing something about it.

In golf it is easy to measure our performance based on how well we perform at different areas of the game. For example an average PGA Tour player would hit 64% of fairways, 65% of greens in regulation, and make 28.5 putts per round. Other helpful statistics are: driving distance, up and down percentage, sand saves, and average putts per green hit in regulation. With the advent of Shotlink the tour can measure every shot a player makes and use it to provide statistical feedback for the players and spectators. Start with the basic statistics and if you feel it is necessary go into more detail. When you know how your performance breaks down, you can begin to work on the parts that are holding you back from your outcome goal. If your example is to become a nine handicap then you can gather statistics of where you are now and what parts of your game need to be improved to get to your outcome goal.

Average score and the key performance factors:

79- 8 GIR, 61% of Fairways, 31.7 putts per round

89- 3 GIR, 36% of Fairways, 35 putts per round

99- 0 GIR, 11% of Fairways, 38.3 putts per round

4. <u>Process goals</u>- what you will do on a consistent basis to improve your standards of performance. This is how are you going to accomplish those performance goals. This is the day to day goals of practicing, taking lessons, and doing whatever is necessary to improve your performance. If your fairways hit are at 40% and your performance goal is to be at 60% you need to figure out how to close that gap. It is not just practicing more, because you could have poor mechanics and by practicing you will just be re-enforcing bad habits. Process goals are about using your time correctly. What needs to be completed on a weekly basis to raise your level of performance? Most people know what is necessary to improve they just haven't been willing to do it.

5. Understand what needs to be <u>sacrificed</u> to pursue these goals. This will identify how committed you are to the process. What are the potential areas you will have to sacrifice in order to pursue your golf

dream? This may be financial. You may need to spend a large amount of money on equipment, lessons, rounds of golf, and practice balls. That money could be spent on something else. The same goes with time. The time that is needed to improve your game to reach your goals could be spent somewhere else. You could spend more time with family, with friends, at your job, or with another hobby. Identify if you have any conflicts with what you may have to sacrifice. If you wait until later you will experience frustration as you try to do everything. I wish I had understood this principle of goal setting because I set myself up for failure when I first turned pro. I thought I would practice eight hours a day and have plenty of time for a job and my wife. I lacked the skill of organizing my time and dealing with the reality of what I could and could not accomplish. I was in constant conflict as I tried to squeeze thirty hours into a twenty-four hour day. This constant conflict with my time eventually led to me to quit competitive golf. I teach players to identify how to realistically schedule practice time and communicate with significant others how your time and money allotment will change as you pursue new goals.

Below is an example of a professional golfer. You can add many more outcome, performance, and process goals to the list so you have as detailed roadmap as possible.

1. Dream to win the U.S. Open

2. Outcome goals- these are measurable, not always in control with golf, time sensitive, provide motivation

   1) Qualify for the PGA tour

   2) Make cut in a PGA tour event

   3) Make the top 10 in a PGA tour event

   4) Win on the PGA tour

3. Performance Goals- define performance gaps- why haven't you reached your outcome goals yet?

Ave. 66% Greens in regulation	Current Level 58%
Ave. 63% of fairways hit	Current Level 55%
Ave. 29 Putts per round	Current Level 31 putts
Ave. 285 yards off of the tee	Current Level 275 yards

4. Process goals- what can you do to improve your performance standards?

Begin a workout program- to get stronger

Improve putting by taking lessons and practicing fifteen hours a week on putting

Do the drills instructor gives to improve takeaway

Practice routine

Practice visualization of swing to improve confidence

I chose to look at a PGA tour player goal to illustrate the ultimate in performance. Your dream is unique; however, you must understand that a dream requires many steps before completion. Take your dream and break it down. By doing so you gain clarity on what is expected and understand the reality of how you are going to do it.

Problems with traditional goal setting:

1. Only focus on dream or outcome- golfer has no idea what the first step is to achievement.

2. Dream/outcome goal is not believed that it can be accomplished. No long-term work will be done if the belief system doesn't match the challenge of the goal.

To make goal setting as powerful as possible you should write out all of your goals. When you write your goals out it helps you see how they can be achieved. Writing them down commits you to them. When goals stay in your head as a wish, not much action is taken. Review your written goals daily if necessary to remind you of what you want to accomplish. Goals can be adjusted as you go along and allow you to be flexible as to when the goals need to be achieved. It is easy to get impatient when you don't reach goals on your timeline. If you stay flexible you will stay focused on pushing forward even if your outcome goals are more challenging to achieve then previous thought. There are numerous stories of players like Tom Lehman who struggled on various mini tours before finally breaking through to PGA Tour success. He went on the win a British Open and became the Ryder Cup captain for the 2006 United States Team. His perseverance allowed him to stay focused on what was necessary to move closer to his dream. His work ethic stayed strong and he realized his dream.

Sharing your goals with supportive people is another way to keep on track. You can even have your support system people make you accountable for your goals by checking in with you about your work ethic. By declaring your goals to others you create motivation through the leverage of wanting to step up and accomplish what you have told others you will do. When I was in high school I created a visualization board of the golfer I wanted to become. On the poster board I cut out pictures of my favorite golfers and motivational sayings. I put it up my bedroom so I was constantly reminded of my dreams.

Goal setting is an ongoing process. Consistently check to see if your outcome goals are still what you want and stay committed to the process goals that will ultimately determine your success. Remember, goals are for what you want to accomplish; make adjustments as you see fit. Identify your goals; write them down, and share them with supportive people and you will be amazed at what you can accomplish.

YOUR SHOT

- What is your ultimate outcome goal? Score under 80

- What other outcome goals need to be reached?

- What level of performance do you need to possess to reach the outcome goals?

- What are you going to do on a consistent basis to improve your performance?

- What needs to be sacrificed to reach your goals?

- Are you willing to commit to reaching your goals?

chapter

BELIEFS

WHAT YOU WILL LEARN:

• How Your Beliefs Affect Your Performance

• Identify Limiting Beliefs

• Changing Your Beliefs

• Create Trust In Your Game

*I think he has more belief in himself, more supreme confidence,
than any golfer ever. He thinks he deserves to win and that he's destined to win.
So he does win. It's written all over him.*
BEN CRENSHAW- ON JACK NICKLAUS

*During my winning streaks I got to the point where I thought
I was never going to lose. Everything was so automatic and so easy.
I was so confident; I felt no one could beat me.*
NANCY LOPEZ

You must always be positive, because your body can only do what your brain sees.
CHI CHI RODRIQUEZ

chapter

(4)

Time and time again, I have witnessed players with high level of talents who didn't reach their potential because of their beliefs. These players would sabotage their performance because they let their limiting beliefs stop them from playing full out. In golf your beliefs are linked to your confidence. Confidence is the intangible that can make or break a golfer achieving his goals.

Beliefs are what we take as being true at any moment. Beliefs guide us in perceiving and interpreting reality. We acquire our beliefs from parents, friends, teachers, society, television, music, our perception of the world, and our experiences. Memories also create beliefs. In golf most people can recall their bad shots after a round, yet find it difficult to recall the good shots. Memories of past golf shots create pictures in our mind. If we replay the bad shots over and over we start to believe this is our current reality.

Here's a Belief Quiz- On a scale from 1 to 5, 1 being strongly disagree and 5 being strongly agree answer the following questions.

1. I almost always believe I will play well.

2. I believe I have the ability to achieve my goals in golf.

3. Most of my imagery before a round is positive on what good could happen.

4. I almost never experience strong negative emotions during a shot.

5. I trust my swing mechanics.

Your answers are your beliefs, whether true or false, these are true to you. If you answered with a 1 or 2 on any of the above statements then those would be limiting beliefs for you to adjust.

Our beliefs of our golf game can sometimes shift into our real life. I experienced this first hand as I linked my golf performance with my identity as a person. This set up a very destructive pattern. If I was playing well, I would think I was a good person. If I played poorly, I would think I was a bad person. The cycle was intensified because most people knew me as Rick the golfer and this perpetuated the idea that my golf game is who I am as a person. This took its toll on me mentally and emotionally, which put even more pressure on my golf performance. I found it difficult to talk to people after a bad round. I would beat myself up with self talk that would tear down my self-esteem. I became depressed when I played poorly because I couldn't separate my golf performance from me as a person.

I quit golf for six months and this changed my perspective. I realized that golf was an activity I had spent time doing, but it wasn't me. I did many other things in my life such as work, school, family, friends, other hobbies like working out and watching football. I was much more than golf and being away from the game taught me this valuable lesson. You don't have to quit golf to realize you are much more than your game. You as a person are greater than any activity you spend your time doing. Golf is a game that can seduce us with its simplicity and we feel we can conquer it. As the game becomes a quest for mastery, we need to separate the person from the game. Our identity is made up of our beliefs about who we are; realize you are someone who plays golf, not a golfer who lives life.

Beliefs relate to our golf performance because they affect how we act. If I choose to believe that I am a poor putter, this will affect me every time I putt. If I choose to believe I am a great ball striker this will affect every time I hit a full shot. Belief and trust go hand in hand. If you don't trust your abilities you have a certain low expectation belief about your level. This trust can be tested on specific shots and in specific situations. I know many golfers who trust their swings on the practice range, yet don't trust their swing on the golf course. What happened? To many golfers, the golf course represents something different than the practice range. This representation affects their belief system. The same is true of golfers who trust their swings on the golf course while playing with friends, yet do not trust their swings during competitive rounds. Again the perception that things have changed triggers different beliefs. Do you think Tiger Woods has different levels of trust in his swing? You either fully trust your swing or you don't.

This is different than trusting certain shots. Each shot is different because of the challenges it possesses. Your job is to realize what the best shot to play is and how you are best able to perform it. People confuse trust with being aggressive on every shot. They start playing low percentage shots and tell me later they trusted their swing. These are two different issues. Trusting your mechanics is one thing, trusting your decision making is another. Later I will cover how to make decisions on the golf course before executing the shot.

Next time you are ready to hit a shot go back and purposely remember the last time you hit this shot well. For most this is difficult because so many are conditioned to remember the bad shots. An exercise at home would be to write down at least one great shot you have hit with each club. Even write down great pitch shots, chip shots, bunker shots, trouble shot, etc. By doing this exercise you will see on paper that you have hit a lot of great golf shots. By using these good memories while playing you will boost your confidence and will change your belief about your game.

I find it interesting how often golfers attempt shots that they believe they can not execute. When you introduce doubt you begin to confuse the mind. Your mind wants to commit fully to an action without doubt getting in the way. Your negative belief starts anticipating negative results and emotions. Hit shots you are confident you can execute. If doubt enters your mind you can choose a different shot or change your belief about the shot you are going to hit.

In the introduction, I wrote about the success equation. Beliefs were the second part of the equation. Beliefs affect your emotional state. I don't know any golfers who play with a lot of doubt who succeed. These players look uneasy on the course. Contrast that with the supreme confidence of Tiger Woods and you see an athlete who carries himself confidently at all times. Belief in your ability to hit a shot will translate into an empowering feeling of confidence. Confidence is the one universal trait that all peak performers possess.

I have learned so much from the thousands of lessons that I have given. One playing lesson taught me more about beliefs than any other. I was taking a beginner out on the golf course for the first time. He had never played on a course before and I wanted to help him with basic etiquette while experiencing a few holes. On our second hole which happened to be a 135 yard par 3, he steps up and makes a hole in one with a 7 iron. I jumped up and down for him telling him what he just accomplished and he looked at me as if I was crazy.

He said, "Why are you getting so excited, isn't that what I am supposed to do, is hit the ball in the hole."

Now I had a dilemma. Did I tell him that he was right to expect that will happen again or do I stress to him how rare it is to make a hole in one even with the most highly skilled player. His perception was simple: get the ball in the hole. He had no judgment on how to do it; he just knew that was the objective of the game. He was playing from a mental state of anything is possible. While 99% of the golfing population play from the mental state of golf is impossible. What is your belief about what is possible on the course?

Beliefs affect:

1. Decision making- you will make different decisions on the course when you are confident versus when you have doubts.

2. Commitment level- when you doubt your ability you fall short from committing fully to the shot at hand.

3. Expectations- when you are confident you begin to expect good things to happen. You know you will play well, so you end up playing well. The opposite happens also, you believe you are in a slump and you expect the slump to continue.

4. Focus- with confidence comes better focus. You can stay focused on your target and your game plan when you are confident. When you have doubts you begin to focus on the trouble and dwell on what could go wrong.

How we can change our beliefs:

1. Identify old beliefs about yourself that you know now are no longer true.

2. Identify current beliefs that:

   o Support you

   o Disempower you

3. Identify what beliefs you need to be the best golfer possible

4. Visualize yourself with these beliefs- in situations when having these empowering beliefs would serve you best. Run these scenarios over and over.

5. Realize your thoughts create your beliefs. We run 95% of the same thoughts through our mind yesterday that we will run today. Become aware of your self-talk, keep track for three rounds what thoughts go through your head. Write down the negative thoughts and the positive thoughts. Which did you have more of? The more you repeat a thought the more likely it will turn into a belief.

6. Reframe negative thoughts (beliefs). Write out challenges to your disempowering beliefs.

   Example- Change "I am a poor putter" to

   "I may not make all my putts, but I have definitely made a lot of putts."

   Or "I can make this putt."

7. The use of affirmations- Affirmations are brief, positive statements that help direct energy, focus, and emotions. Write down the desired belief that will replace the current belief. Affirmations can also be repeated as self-talk or said out loud as a way to shift beliefs.

8. Self-hypnosis- similar to affirmations, yet said in a state of relaxation. Hypnosis is geared to change your subconscious mind, which is more powerful than your conscious mind. The subconscious constitutes 86% of your mind, with conscious mind only 14%, yet we try to change the conscious mind through willpower and will fail if the subconscious mind does not support the conscious minds directions. Your subconscious mind responds to repetition in a relaxed state. The use of audio programs that get you into this state are popular with elite athletes as a way to relax the mind and reprogram beliefs.

9. Act as if- this will be explained in the chapter about emotions. Acting as if will for that moment suspend your belief system. I have taught golf to actors who take on different roles. The skill of acting as someone else is a powerful technique that golfers can use to tap into a confident state. How would you act if you were confident of your golfing ability? Now start acting that way.

Our language defines our reality. Unfortunately most people use language to perpetuate negative beliefs about themselves. Our internal dialogue will strengthen beliefs we have about ourselves. The ability to become aware of our self-talk is the first step. Reframing language in a positive way will have a powerful impact on your belief system. Look at how you talk about things. When I am working with clients I am aware of their language. I sometimes challenge the language so the golfer becomes aware of what he is saying. A common example is the statement, "I always miss putts." I would then challenge that statement by saying, "Always?" This stops the golfer to realize that always is inaccurate. It may be true that there have been certain times that you missed an important putt, but by saying "always" you are undermining your confidence with a statement that is false. Your subconscious doesn't know the difference between what is true or false, just what you tell it to be. Day to day you need to talk to yourself in a positive way. Clarify what you want and tell yourself you are going to reach your goal. The subconscious will then follow.

How we judge each shot and each round will strengthen our beliefs. Become aware of you emotional judgments to shots. The more emotion you pour into the judgment the stronger the belief will become. So, on great shots get excited and tell yourself what a great shot you hit! On poor shots, learn from them and leave the shot in a neutral state.

How many times after a round has someone asked you how you played and your answer was, "I played ok, missed some putts, hit a few bad drives;" I never hear someone respond with, "I played great; I hit a lot of good shots and enjoyed the day." Golfers have a difficult time admitting when they play well and seem to think if they admit they played well that they will be judged. Also, golfers like to tell everyone the reasons why they didn't play well and make excuses for the poor play. I don't like excuses. I used to make excuses all the time as a junior golfer. My poor performance was always blamed on the bumpy greens, slow play, playing partners, and the weather. Without taking responsibility for my game I didn't improve. Once I stopped telling those "stories" I finally took charge of my game. It was me who swung the club and made the decisions that shaped my game. What I learned was twofold: (1) Take responsibility for my game and (2) Admit when I am playing well because it boosts my confidence. If you don't take responsibility you will never get better and if you always downplay your performance your confidence will suffer.

Think as if you were your own caddy. If you have the chance to caddy for someone else or have a caddy yourself, do it. One can learn so much from having a caddy. I ask my clients how a caddy would react if you hit a poor shot. As the caddy, would you tell the player they choked or would you say let's get it back on the next shot. Of course, it would be the latter. However, when we don't have a caddy do we treat ourselves with the same attitude after a poor shot? Usually the golfer beats him or herself up with negative self-talk. Next time on the course pretend you are your own caddy and see how that changes your beliefs and self-talk. You will find you will remain much more positive and ready for the next shot.

> *I think that your mind will carry you. The mind controls the body.*
> *So if the mind tells the body what to do, it'll do it. It's just a matter*
> *of getting the mind under control to make your body respond.*
> **TIGER WOODS**

I love the people who push us to think outside our comfort zone. One of my favorites is Pia Nilsson a golf coach who has worked with many great golfers, including Annika Sorenstam. She tries to instill in her students the belief that they can shoot 54. That would be getting a birdie on every hole of a par 72 hole course. She is changing the mindset of her students by having them believe that anything is possible. Knowing your comfort zone will tell you what your beliefs are about your golf game.

When a golfer combines a certain expectation of ability with a likely score, a comfort zone is created. This becomes very apparent when a golfer starts a round better than they ever have before. If an eighteen-handicap golfer starts with five straight pars this may trigger the golfer to think about the future and what might be a career low. Usually such a golfer will "come back to reality" by hitting poor shots and finish with very near the same score shot in previous rounds. The best golfers push their comfort zone out so far that _anticipation_

they feel comfortable when the round is going really well. Most average golf-ers will feel uncomfortable with a great start. Their comfort zone or expecta-tion of their ability doesn't match this great performance and they will find a way to get back to being comfortable. This means hitting poor shots. Your score matches your expectation of your abilities.

Comfort zones revolve around career best scores or certain score levels like breaking 100, 90, 80, par, and 70 for the first time. These scores become goals. However if we get nervous or don't believe we can break through we will sabotage our good starts. How many times have we experienced a great front nine and a poor back nine? In these cases we actually feel uncomfort-able playing well. We start to question it, thinking it won't last. Guess what? It doesn't. We shoot poorly on the back nine. The process goal is to get excited about playing well and embrace this good performance. Golfers work so hard to shoot lower scores, yet when they actually are doing it they can't control their thinking. Their thinking becomes negative and what was an easy game of golf turns into a struggle. The thinking needs to stay as present as possible. Stay with your routine and break down your round into mini goals. It is easy to get ahead of yourself, so concentrating on the present is the first step. Next, I would encourage golfers who are pushing their comfort zone to play aggres-sively. Most will play conservatively and hope to not make a mistake. When you're playing well you are in the mindset of wanting to hit good shots, not thinking about where you don't want the ball to go.

When golfers are challenging their best score the first area to be aware of is self talk. If golfers say to themselves that the reason they're playing well is because of luck or this level of performance won't last long they're setting themselves up for a fall. Stay positive with statements like, "Keep it going, stay focused on this shot" or "this is fun, let's make some more pars." Your self-talk relates back to your belief system. I have seen golfers play great and then their playing partners mention how well they are playing, causing them to analyze their round and realize that they are playing a lot better than nor-mal. Remember to be aware of your self-talk and turn negative self-talk into positive performance cues to keep you in the present. Staying present is about what is in your control. When we think ahead of the potential scoring sce-narios, we shift our thinking to what is out of our control. By thinking of your routine and using positive self-talk we focus on what is in our control, the present moment.

Golfers tell me all the time they want to be better players and some of my clients tell me they want to be great players. Wanting something and believing something are two different things. Are your beliefs in line with what you want to achieve? That internal belief of your present ability and future potential is key for long-term motivation. Cultivating the belief that you will achieve the goal is crucial to accomplishing it. I would rather work with golfers with total belief in their ability to achieve their goal than with players with more talent who don't believe they will succeed. Believing in your ability will keep you going when the results have not materialized. Those who believe in themselves will better deal with inevitable slumps. We have all achieved great things in our life; remind yourself of those times when you kept going despite the struggles. It doesn't have to be golf related.

By remembering your past successes, you will build your self-belief in you as a person. Start believing in the ability you currently have and the belief that your game will improve in the future.

When golfers start playing better you'll have to start dealing with the new expectations other will place upon you. As your handicap goes down and you start shooting career best scores others will definitely treat you differently. Some people start feeling uncomfortable with the expectations of other people. You have to have a definite belief that you are a good player and will not allow others' beliefs detract from your performance. Playing better is everyone's goal, yet there are different perceptions to good golf.

Some perceive good golf as a lucky event that won't repeat itself for a long time. While others play well and realize their hard work is paying off. Good golfers use good rounds to build their belief that they are good, poor golfers never admit that they can actually play well. It is okay to admit you played well. As a rule people feel uncomfortable admitting they are good at things. Yet the best know they are great and usually will display that attitude to others through their language and how they carry themselves.

Some sports psychology coaches view expectations of positive outcomes as negative because they cause pressure to increase and frustration to set in when expectations are not met. However, I want my clients to have realistic expectations that the hard work they are putting in will result in lower scores. Why else would we practice and take lessons? We do these things to play better. The problem arises when the expectations are based on false evidence and are unrealistic. The classic example is the golfer who takes one golf lesson and practices once on the range. This golfer comes back to the golf instructor disappointed in a score that wasn't five shots better than previous outings. A consistent work ethic will produce positive results. The best players expect to play well every time they tee it up. If they don't play well they have the mental skills to deal with the poor play and still make the most of it. Do not lower your expectations. What you begin to do is accept a lower standard for your play. I want you to push yourself. I want you to set high standards, work accordingly, and expect to play well. Holding yourself to a high standard is very empowering. A standard may be to commit yourself to each shot you hit that round. Another standard could be to stay emotionally calm no matter the result of a given shot. Expect that you will play to these standards and let the outcome of score be a result of your new standards.

It is difficult to tell people to not have any expectations while playing. Everyone plays golf for certain reasons and to fulfill those reasons is a positive experience not a negative one. When you become complacent and don't expect the best from yourself you often get below average play. There have been times when golfers play well when they have no expectations of results. This may occur after a long break from the game or when a golfer plays a difficult course for the first time. What has really happened is the player has adjusted expectations according to the present challenge.

An unrealistic expectation is the desire to hit the ball perfectly. When you define a shot as perfect it sets the golfer up for failure. How many shots have you hit perfectly in one round of golf? Even top pros may say that they have hit four shots perfectly in one round of golf. That is the best of the best. Remember I want you to expect good shots, not necessarily perfect shots. The key is how you deal with results that don't match your expectations. If your criteria for good shots are only perfect shots then that is a built in problem of constant unmatched expectations. The champions expect the best, yet understand that not every single shot will be up to their standards. The best react by saying, "I missed that shot, I will make the next one."

When the expectation of a certain score is the only focus then performance can suffer, especially early in a round when it starts poorly. The secret is to take your outcome expectations and break them down to the process that is needed to reach that expectation. If I expect to shoot par on a given day then I also must expect that I will be the type of player who can shoot that score. It may seem like semantics, however, I expect myself to focus at a certain level, manage my emotions, and make committed decisions. When I do execute those skills to the level of a scratch player then I have set myself up to fulfill my outcome goal of shooting par. Think about what you have in your control and what is out of your control. That day you can control your level of focus, how you carry yourself, and how committed you are to your shots. What is out of your control is how the ball bounces. That's why a target score can have a negative affect because focusing on the outcome goal of par score can cause undo pressure and create frustration when you start poorly. If one starts off well the golfer then might go into protect mode. Shooting your best rounds is about task process, not outcome goals. Expect yourself to execute the process of the shot. The fine line between expectations and standards is crucial to understand.

A tough expectation to deal with is the introduction of competition. We would all love to win the next tournament or beat our group this weekend. Expecting to accomplish this goal can be a deterrent. There can only be one winner and golf is a sport where we lose more than we win. Even Tiger Woods has lost more tournaments than he has won. This gets back to what is in your control and what is out of your control.

I had a client who wanted to win a junior tournament and expected to win the tournament. He told me the competition was weak and this was going to be his time to finally win. The problem with this was twofold. He was underestimating his competition and he was putting too much pressure on the outcome. What ended up happening is he shot a very good round of golf, but lost to another player who had a career round. We talked about how he felt. He was disappointed in that he didn't win. Even though he played well he couldn't control what the other players shot. We shifted his awareness back to how he played and that changed how he felt. Instead of staying disappointed, he could be proud of his performance. A goal of winning a specific tournament can help motivate you to practice and get you excited to play. Wanting to win and expecting to win are different. Ask yourself a better question, how do I need to carry myself on the golf course to give myself the best chance to win?

Remember you are playing a game. Do you play golf because you love the game and the enjoyment it brings? If our expectations are purely score driven, then our enjoyment is just based on the score on a given hole or round. The biggest drawback will be to those golfers who do have high expectations and who don't know how to deal with not meeting them.

Start today to strengthen your beliefs about your game. Check your self-talk to hear if you are using supportive language or critical words. Play back those great shots that you have had in the past. Adjust your goals for the round to what is in your control and measure your expectations to make sure that it will empower you instead of distract you. Choose today to believe you can accomplish your goals and pull off the next shot. No matter the situation it is your choice on what you believe you can and can not do. Start believing!

YOUR SHOT

- What belief do you have about your game that is detrimental to your performance?

- Which technique will you use to create supportive beliefs about your game?

- Be aware of your self-talk and begin to talk to yourself as a supportive caddy would

- Only create expectations for what is under your control; what standards will you commit to?

chapter

EMOTIONS

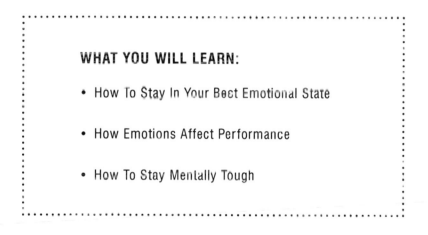

WHAT YOU WILL LEARN:

• How To Stay In Your Best Emotional State

• How Emotions Affect Performance

• How To Stay Mentally Tough

To control your mind and body throughout a round of golf with all its pressures and frustrations is probably the single biggest challenge in golf.
GREG NORMAN

A bad attitude is worse than a bad swing.
PAYNE STEWART

I've been nervous all week. Now I'm just bloody terrified.
TONY JACKLIN- before the final round of the 1969 British Open- which he won

Fear ruins more golf shots, for duffer and star, than any other one factor.
TOMMY ARMOUR

chapter

5

A tense mind breeds tense muscles, and tense muscles
make you feel clumsy, out of gear.
JACK NICKLAUS

Just because you're nervous doesn't mean you can't hit great shots.
PAUL AZINGER

Golf is a unique game in which you are supposed to be in control of your emotions to play your best. Sport psychology coaches have professed the importance of not getting too high or too low emotionally. The problem with this teaching is in the development of young players who show no emotion and no personality on the course. Golf is something to be experienced not by acting numb, but being fully engaged in the process. You will learn that your best emotional state to play is different than someone else's.

The lack of emotional control has ruined many golf careers, both competitive and recreational. Most of the time the emotions of anger, frustration, and disappointment affect performance negatively. I enjoy experiencing the different emotions a round of golf produces. The trick is to find what emotions work for you and which emotions don't. The intensity of the emotion has more effect than the actual emotion itself. I have seen several players who will use a negative emotion to kick start a great performance and have seen other players play in a daze and never play well.

Emotions are basically feelings associated with a specific stimulus. Our perceptions of our surroundings make up our reality. We then label these things and create emotions that are tied to certain beliefs about these things. Your thoughts become beliefs and your beliefs will elicit an emotional response. If I ask you, how good of a player are you?" Your response would be your belief and it would be tied to an emotion. If you say, "I am a poor player" compared to "I am a great player," you will feel different depending on which belief you hold. Emotions will affect the way you make decisions and execute your swing.

I used to play golf angry and it affected my tempo and feel for the game. I would hit another poor shot and the anger would intensify. Emotions can help or destroy your golf performance. Emotions are not necessarily bad for your golf game. There have been great players who have shown emotion on the course such as Seve Ballesteros and Tiger Woods. These players use emotions in a positive way. If not controlled, emotions can cause difficulty in performing their best.

An observation I have made regarding Tiger's emotional intensity after making a birdie or great shot has decreased since he first came on tour. Tiger still gets excited, but he doesn't pump his fists as hard or stomp off the greens with the same aggression. He realized that it was a challenge to get his emotional state back to the place it needed to be to hit his next shot. If we are too pumped up our body will respond with a faster heart rate, faster breathing rate, which will affect the rhythm of your swing.

Most of the current professionals look like robots. They are doing this to stay emotionally stable during a round so they can be consistent. But a word of warning, don't try to completely turnoff your emotions. We play this game because it makes us feel certain ways. I play golf for the challenge and if I hit a good shot I want to allow myself to celebrate it with a fist pump.

Show me the fellow who walks calmly after topping a drive or missing a kick-in putt, showing the world he's under perfect control,
yet burning up inside, and I'll show you one who's going to lose.
If you bottle up anger entirely, it poisons your control centers.
SAM SNEAD

Your game is a beast, and either you can control the beast or the beast can control you. As you get more experience competing, you develop better ways of coping with your feelings. If I'm a little too charged up, I take a long, deep breath.
SEVE BALLESTEROS

What emotions serve you best in playing golf? The common answers are the emotional states of confidence and trust, while staying focused, calm, and relaxed. These emotional states; are feelings that affect you both physically and mentally. If I am in a confident state my body will respond differently than if I am in a relaxed state. You know what state is best for you to play in and it revolves around the emotions that you experience on the golf course.

What emotions destroy your golf performance? The common answers are doubt, frustration, fear, scattered focus, and anger. These negative emotions create disempowering states which affect your body. These states affect how your mind and body react. Emotions change the state of your body. The body then responds to them by adjusting such factors as tension, heart rate, and breathing rate. What negative emotions are you experiencing on the golf course?

Emotions have negative effects on performance:

- Inability to narrow focus when necessary

- Mind gets busier and decision making is impaired

- Can cause self-talk to get more negative

- Creates physical tension which impedes ability to hit shots

Knowing I've practiced effectively to strengthen my game
gives me added confidence on the course.
TOM LEHMAN

Confidence in your ability allows your brain and nervous system to perform the skills you have practiced and mastered. This part is related to conscious competence; we know we can do it and we do it. The zone is the next level of unconscious competence, allowing you to be in the moment that you just execute. Confidence is a given and allows you to be on autopilot. Your perception of the situation creates an emotion. This emotion or feeling interacts with your body and changes the body's chemistry. The body now is asked to perform a task (hitting a golf shot) with a different body state than it had practiced being in before. This constant change in emotional state leads to inconsistency. This is what affects the player who is great on the range, but plays poorly on the course. The major reason why is that this golfer plays at two different emotional states. On the range they are at their optimal performance state but when they step on to the first tee their state changes. They haven't practiced in this state so they will perform differently.

You can win tournaments when you're mechanical, but golf is a game of emotion and adjustment. If you're not aware of what's happening to your mind and your body when you're playing, you'll never be able to be the very best you can be.
JACK NICKLAUS

The best golfers know at what arousal level they play best. This is related to the pressure an individual feels and how it affects his performance. The trick is to find what level of arousal is ideal for you and how to get into that level. Arousal level is a physical process of tension and adrenaline. We can perform between a completely relaxed state or a completely excited state. Emotions do come into play; however you need to realize what physical state in which you play your best golf in. On a scale of 1 (sleeping) to 10 (extreme excitement), where do you play your best golf? When I ask this question of my clients they answer as if guessing what the right answer is, so they say 3 meaning relaxed. As a group, golfers think that being relaxed is the best arousal state to play your best. As I probe for the answer, I find when someone really played his best his arousal level was closer to 5 or 6. One such player said he played best when slightly on edge; a little anticipation and a spring in his step. It was not a relaxed state. I bring this up because many golfers have read books or magazine articles teaching that to play your best golf you must be relaxed. This generality is misleading. It is true many players do not play well when they get too tight or excited, but the answer may not be to be relaxed. Lowering your arousal level from 8 to 5 would be enough to gain physical control back and play great golf. Being too relaxed can be detrimental. Golfers who are too relaxed find themselves getting bored or taking shots for granted. Being focused and at your optimal arousal state is the secret to peak performance.

Different shots require different arousal states. For putting, chipping, pitching, it is best to have a slightly lower arousal level, around a 4. With these types of shots it requires fine motor skills and your sense of feel needs to be at its best. When you want to hit a driver on a long par 4 you may swing your best with an elevated arousal level at 7. I know hitting a driver with full speed requires my body to be in a different arousal state than hitting a flop shot over a bunker and trying to land it soft. That is why managing your emotions and arousal state is the key to peak performance.

There are physiological changes associated with an arousal state. These changes would be in heart rate, muscle tension, blood pressure, and brain waves. I have a device called the Peak Achievement Trainer that measures brain wave activity and is a useful biofeedback tool. The device hooks on your head like ear phones with sensors that go on your forehead and earlobes. The impulses are registered and are shown on the computer. When golfers use this tool, they are amazed their best focus is in a state of alertness and a sense of calm. When the individual becomes frustrated, the brainwaves jumped; when the individual becomes quiet the brainwaves went down and stabilized.

Understanding how expectations for your game can affect your arousal level will help you control the outcome of your game. It's important to have high standards for your game and to expect to control your emotional state, and it is your responsibility to maintain your optimal performance state. What we can't control is how the ball bounces; however, we can control how we react emotionally to the shot. Having performance expectations is slightly different because those expectations are out of your control. When the outcome we expect is not met some will get discouraged, frustrated, or even angry. This will change the arousal level in the player. For instance, if a player expects to win a tournament and is playing well, but his playing partner is shooting lower this can create an arousal problem. Performance will change, usually for the worse. Having expectations can help motivate players; however, it sometimes places too much emphasis on the outcome instead of the process, which is in the player's control.

The Masters is a perfect example of how the pressure of golf- and the buildup about how important it is- can change you so that you hardly know yourself.
JOE INMAN

I get too jazzed up. The first round has killed me for fifteen straight years.
JOHNNY MILLER- ON THE MASTERS

You need to find ways for you to regulate your arousal level. Here are some keys to getting back into your optimal arousal state:

- Monitor your heart rate- Check it in the morning, check it during a practice session, and check it during a competitive round. This is one step of awareness.

- Create process goals for your round, built around awareness of arousal level. An example would be, I will check how my body feels on every shot.

- Avoid caffeine and other stimulants before and during a round

- Create habits of checking in with body tension throughout a normal day.

- Practice deep breathing, rolling shoulders, yoga, and meditation to decrease body tension.

The goal is to identify:

1. The best emotional state at which you perform. On the 1 to 10 scale, do you play best closer to a 1 (extremely relaxed) or closer to a 10 (extremely excited)?

2. Understanding how your arousal level changes depending on your perception of the situation. Be aware of your perception of what a shot means and change your perception if it causes you to get out of your optimal arousal level. If you normally get very angry after you miss-hit a shot, change the reaction to what can you learn from that shot. You control your thoughts which control your emotions. Start responding to your golf shots in ways that will maintain your emotional state.

3. How to change your emotional state when it is not serving your performance.

Ways we can change our emotional state:

1. Write out your best and worst golf experience

   o Identify the positive emotions that you possessed at your best

   o Identify the negative emotions that you possessed at your worst

   o Realize you have played some great golf and your emotional state was crucial to your performance

2. Visualization

   o See yourself in the emotional state you feel is the best for you to play your best

   o See yourself in the arousal level you play your best at

   o See yourself making adjustments in your emotional state when you feel you would be out of your comfort zone

3. Breathing

   o With proper breathing you can begin to control your body's reactions to your emotions

   o Breathing changes what you focus on, thus changes perception of the situation

Correct breathing is done from the diaphragm. The breath should be deep and controlled. Many golfers have had success with a breathing tempo of inhaling to a count of 4, holding for a count of 2, and exhaling to a count of 8. This combination will insure a full breath and will slow you down.

4. Centering technique- use breathing and awareness of your body to create emotional stability. Bring your attention to a specific point on your body, like just below your navel and keep your focus on that point as you breathe. This will slow down your body and slow down your mind. Centering literally brings you back to the present and gives you a new starting point to move forward from.

5. Using your physiology to change emotional state quickly

   o How you walk, talk, stand affects your emotional state.

   o Pretend you are fearful- how would you stand and breathe? What would your facial expressions be?

   o Pretend you are confident- how would you stand, breathe? What would your facial expressions be?

   o Model the best. I have seen Tiger Woods play several times in person and love how he carries himself. He walks in such a way that you know by just looking at him that he is supremely confident and ready to play. If you get a chance to see Tiger play in person, do it. Then start to copy how he walks. You will feel differently.

6. Body awareness- scan your body for tension to help regulate being at your best emotional state. You may find your hands clenched or your neck tight. The first step is by stopping and checking your physical state. You then can make the necessary adjustments with the other techniques.

A technique to help with body tension is Progressive Muscle Relaxation. This occurs when a golfer tenses and relaxes various muscle groups throughout the body while focusing on the feelings associated with relaxation and being aware of the state. This technique is best done at home when you can go through each muscle group slowly and purposely. On the course you could simply tighten your fist as tight as possible for 10 seconds and then release the fist. You will instantly feel relaxed after that exercise.

7. Autogenic Suggestions: The golfer learns to relax his/her mind and body in response to verbal commands. Specific statements are repeated over and over as the golfer concentrates on different body parts. The statements might be "warm and heavy" or "calm and cool." These words can then be used as reminders on the golf course to trigger relaxation.

These techniques can be used to:

o Calm down

o Manage your energy level

o Refocus

o Help you sleep

o Control Stress

o To facilitate visualization training

ANCHORING

Wouldn't it be great if we could recapture the wonderful shots of our past and use them to boost our confidence at any time? There is a fantastic technique called anchoring that can accomplish such a feat. The goal of anchoring is to store and then trigger resourceful feelings and thoughts on the golf course. An anchor is a neurological association between a specific stimulus and a response. An example would be hearing a song you haven't heard in twenty years that brings you back to that time you heard it or seeing a high school friend at a reunion and remembering all the great times you had together. In golf anchors occur when getting to your least favorite hole and stepping on the tee box triggers the negative memories of past poor performance. The opposite experienced is when you step onto your favorite hole and remember all the great shots you have hit. These are unconscious connections and these responses are felt in many different situations on the golf course. I have worked with some very good players who create anxiety every time they have short par putts. These same golfers feel no anxiety on short birdie putts. Your perception of the shot creates your reality. You respond according to how you think about each shot. Sometimes you feel different even though you didn't have a conscious thought about the shot. Our memories are strong. The memory triggers an image which in turn triggers an emotional response. If you don't change the perception you will keep responding the same way. Most golfers have more negative triggers than positive. The goal of using the anchoring technique is to consciously control your emotional response at any given moment.

A trigger could be linked to any of your senses. Most triggers in golf are visual. A trigger can be anything from seeing a particular hole, to having to hit a particular shot. Golfers have shared with me that just seeing a particular playing partner has created a negative reaction. The link of what you see and what you feel is the anchor. Let's create powerful anchors that link positive emotions to once negative triggers. For this exercise I want you to think of an anchor that can represent an empowering emotion such as confidence. Most golfers like to use the anchor of making a fist as an empowering anchor. For example if your anchor is to make a fist this would trigger you to feel the emotional response of confidence. By linking confidence with the fist you have created a powerful tool to help you when you need the emotional shift. To create this empowering anchor you need to go through an imagery exercise The first question to answer is what emotional state do you want to elicit or on call at any moment on the golf course? A majority of golfers say they want to elicit confidence. Next you want to recall a specific occasion in the past when you have been in that state. Relive that specific experience as vividly as possible. What were you seeing, feeling, hearing, tasting during that experience? Like turning up the volume on your radio, I want you to turn the intensity of this powerful emotion way up. Once you are in the peak of that empowering emotional state it is time to set the anchor. If your anchor is making a fist then this is the time to make a fist while you are imagining the past peak experience. Do this exercise over and over by recalling other positive experiences when you felt confidence.

Set the anchor when you are feeling that peak state. This is called stacking the anchor. You are taking your past positive experiences and bringing them together in one place on your body, in this case your fist. The fist has now stored the memories and positive emotions. To feel the positive emotion in the present all you have to do is fire the anchor which is making a fist.

Anchors need to be:

- Intense- a peak emotional state

- Timed- setting the anchor at the highest emotional point

- Unique- a location that is not used often

- Replicable- use the anchor in the exact way as it was set

- Frequency- the more times you set the anchor the stronger the connection

I learned this technique after my competitive days and found that it was powerful and so easy to use. My anchor is when I place my thumb and forefinger of my right hand together. I use this anchor on all my shots to remind me of the confident feeling I want for the next shot. I fire the anchor in my pre-shot routine right before I approach the ball. Experiment with what works for you. Do the exercise and use it. Now it won't matter what triggers you experience on the course, you will have set an anchor that can switch your focus and your emotional state in seconds.

Emotional state is related to the study by optimal performance expert Mihaly Csikszentmihalyi in his book, *Flow: The Psychology of Optimal Experience*. He found that when you're engaged in an activity that commands all of your attention, your concentration sometimes becomes so intense that the rest of the world seems to drop away, and you have a feeling of effortless control. You enjoy the moment and it becomes a peak experience. This is very much the same as the zone. The key part of flow is the skills versus challenge equation. This explains why certain situations cause us stress, while other situations create boredom.

The zone is the term coined by athletes and coaches alike to label that mystical experience of peak performance. The difficult aspect of the zone is teaching it so athletes can tap into this experience more often. The flow state is very similar and has been studied extensively. The flow state occurs when there is a perceived balance between the challenges of the situation and the capabilities of the person to meet the demands of the task. A study by N.B. Stambulova from the P.F. Lesgaft State Academy of Physical Education in St. Petersburg, Russia (Research Quarterly for Exercise and Sport; 3/1/2004;

Clark, Betsy) found that the keys to getting into flow revolved around confidence level and perception of skills.

The key finding is the perception of skills, not necessarily the actual skills. Your perception is your reality. If you think you are a poor putter you will not handle putting challenges the same way as someone who thinks they are a great putter. The reality might be you are a better putter than the person who thinks they are great. The problem is you will respond to the challenge with anxiety, while the other golfer will respond with confidence. That golfer now has a better chance of experiencing flow. Have it become a priority to change your negative perceptions of your skills.

Most golfers, especially better players, are tougher on themselves when it comes to evaluating their golf skills. The two handicap golfer is more inclined to tell me that they are a poor putter than the twenty handicap golfer who might say they are okay at putting. The reality is the two-handicap golfer is better than the twenty-handicap golfer, but begins to compare himself against the best. What this does is change their confidence level, thus changing their ability to perform. Be realistic with your skills, but do not diminish the skills you do have.

- When the perceived challenge is greater than your perceived skill, you will feel anxious.

- When your perceived skill is much greater than the perceived challenge, you will feel bored.

- When your perceived skill matches perceived challenge (or when challenge is a bit beyond skill level) we have a better chance to be in the flow.

If we know we can do it; this will lead to a better emotional state.

Do not be ashamed of choking... any golfer who has never choked on the golf course should be in an asylum... sooner or later all normal human beings encounter situations on the course that they are not, at that particular moment, emotionally capable of handling.
PAUL RUNYAN

Choking is simply, at a specific moment, perceiving a skill level that doesn't match the perceived challenge. This creates an emotional reaction that changes how the physical body performs. The key word is perceived because we have seen it all the time where a player is leading a tournament after three rounds and then "chokes" in the fourth round and shoots a high score. The player perceives the challenge of winning a tournament to be much greater than the perceived skills required to do it, whether that is true or not.

When you develop the confidence in your ability you will strengthen your chances of staying in the optimal performance state even when challenges increase. The challenge of a situation can be embraced with confidence or fueled by doubt. Your perception of the situation is the vital first step of what emotional state you will be in. Look for ways to perceive a situation in an empowering way in order to be in your optimal performance state.

SLUMP

A golfer in a self described slump frequently seeks out a sports psychology coach. A "slump" is a duration of time when performance is declining. Some golfers define a slump as two bad rounds in a row; others only when their scoring average has increased significantly after an entire year. The first thing you must understand is that the only way you can be in a slump is if you believe you are in a slump. This may sound like a play on words, but it is very important to realize that if you use the word "slump" to describe your game then that is exactly what you will have created. I remember the times that Tiger Woods changed his swing and did not play at the same exceptional level we were all accustomed to seeing from him. In all of the interviews during that time Tiger never admitted that his game was in a slump. He would say that he knew the process of change would need some time to make happen. Tiger would go on by saying how "close" he felt; he was raising his game to an even higher level than before the changes. Tiger always stays positive and stays committed to his plan. The average golfer presses the panic button way too soon and creates anxiety that will cause even poorer performance. Attitude is the first thing to check when you feel you are in a slump.

The second area to check is fundamentals. Get back to training by using your fundamentals and make the necessary adjustments. When someone is slumping they jump from swing thought to swing thought instead of getting back to basics. When performance is declining a golfer should place focus on the process of making good swings, not the outcome of a swing. This requires a golfer to get back to focusing on a pre-shot routine that gets one in the present. Another way to get out of a slump is to return to past successes. Remember that you have played good golf and let those positive memories remind you of what has worked.

In my college days, I discovered taking time off could be very helpful when performance is down. Getting away from the game for a couple of weeks or more can refresh your attitude and change your perspective. I have also changed equipment to give me a new start. I am not suggesting that after every bad round you buy a new set of clubs but changing putters or driver can be a switch that can benefit you.

Take responsibility for your actions. I used to have a very hot temper on the golf course as a junior. I usually blamed the course or my playing partners for my outbursts. I didn't take responsibility for my behavior, thus it didn't change until much later. Once I knew that I was the one who controlled my emotions I began to mature on the golf course and my scores started to come down.

What is happening in the rest of your life will affect your emotional state on the golf course. Most people have a difficult time not bringing their other life stresses to the golf course. What happens is loss of focus and a short fuse in dealing with poor shots. You can use the time on the course as your own place to get away from life. Be selfish on the course and stay focused on what you can do while playing to have the most enjoyment. I have clients that are emotionally drained from school, business, or family pressures who are still able to be at their emotional best on the course. It takes experience to separate life from a round of golf. Understand your life stressors that change your emotional state on the golf course. If it is under your control, do something about it; if it is out of your control forget it!

A great way to acquire any skill or trait is by practicing. Practicing your optimal emotional state can be accomplished through visualization. Start this exercise by seeing yourself handling the most difficult situations on a golf course. For some it might be a 3-putt, others it is hitting the ball in the water, while others it could be losing a match. See yourself handling the situation in a positive way. One of the many powerful factors of the technique of visualization is that you can play many different scenarios around in your head and actually practice your emotional reaction. Purposely see yourself react in positive ways to what was once a challenge. Remember your emotional state will lead to a change in behavior. Practice a different emotional state and you will behave differently and your results will change in the process.

The toughest thing for most people to learn in golf is to accept bad holes-
and then forget about them.
GARY PLAYER

BOUNCE BACK- PERSPECTIVE IS THE DIFFERENCE

We all face obstacles on and off the golf course. Those who deal with them in a positive way have the best chance to overcome them. It starts with our perception of the situation; some see a bunker shot as nearly impossible, while others enjoy it and know they can do it. Our perception is built around past memories, our belief system, and our current emotional state. Too often golfers only remember the bad shots. They don't believe they can really pull a shot off, and they become frustrated. They then wonder why the shot didn't come off. The champion golfers live in the present moment and actually use poor play to motivate their performance, instead of detract from it.

Under the most extreme circumstances, when the competition is that fierce and that heightened and my concentration is that high, I feel like I can make things happen. Over the course of my golf career, I've had it happen enough times where I can always say to myself, 'I've done this, I've done it before.' That gives you confidence.
TIGER WOODS

MENTAL TOUGHNESS VERSUS TANKING

There is one distinction between champions and the rest and it is the ability to keep going when the going gets tough. So often I see very talented golfers quit on the course because the round is not going their way. When I say quit it doesn't necessarily mean walking off the course (which I have seen). It is more an attitude of not trying to perform at one's best. This is called tanking. Tanking is the emotional state when you stop trying, make excuses, and just go through the motions. The problem with tanking is that it becomes a habit. If you allow yourself to tank during one round, the next time you face a little adversity you will be more likely to tank again. This process continues until you find yourself only trying if your round starts well.

When your results are poor in a round, the trick is to switch your focus. When the score is the only goal it is easy to give up and say "today is not my day I won't even come close to shooting my handicap, so it doesn't matter." When you hear yourself say this you must switch goals for the rest of the round. The first way is to get back to the process of making each shot important. This means challenging yourself to stay present. Second, focus on getting your swing back by focusing on what produces your best swings. Notice, I didn't say focus on what you are doing wrong; this places your mind in an analytical mindset. Your best swings are most likely in balance, with smooth tempo, and within yourself. Focus on past successes to regain the good form you know you possess.

Third, challenge yourself and change your outcome goal for the rest of the round. If you normally shoot 85 and shot 50 on the front nine a goal for the back could be 43. Starting fresh can change your attitude and give your mind a new target to shoot for. Staying committed to going through your process whether if you are playing poorly or great takes discipline but it should become habitual. Raise your standards to the type of competitor you want to be and see that even your worst will still be better because you made the best of the round. This thinking leads to the mental toughness that the greats possess and that characteristically push them in tough competitions. The mentally tough golfer will prevail over the habitual tanking golfer when they are competing against each other. Decide to become mentally tough and you will surprise yourself in what you will accomplish.

Tanking is not choking. Tanking is mentally quitting, while choking is not having the mental skills to deal with a pressure situation. Golfers who choke are still trying to focus and execute; they just are in an emotional state of confusion and self-imposed pressure. Tanking is worse than choking because it shows weak mental skills. You will avoid the times you choke by learning the skills in this book. Tanking is a choice of giving up when the situation is tough. Tanking is a breakdown in motivation, in that you stop taking action for a desired goal. To stop tanking you need to motivate yourself to step up and perform even though you don't like the results. I am proud of my clients who stick out a poor round and give each shot a 100%. They will use that experience to help them in future rounds when they need to be mentally tough.

Momentum in golf is powerful and we have all experienced a ride on the bogey train. Making a long putt can change our outlook on the next tee, while missing an easy putt can bring our emotional state down. On the first tee we all start with a clean slate, yet as the round goes on we ride the emotional roller coaster up and down depending on the result of the last shot. This roller coaster becomes a train going out of control if we are not aware of it. A lot of players let a bogey or worse affect their emotional state for the next shot. Remember your emotional state contributes to performance. Your emotional state is up to you. You choose how you will react to what happens to you.

Ways to get off the bogey train: get back to basics:

- Stay with your plan for the next hole- don't try to be a hero and risk hitting a shot you know you don't have to make up for the last hole.

- Reframe the situation as a wake up call, not as a time to get down.

- Get back to simple swing thoughts like rhythm and balance.

- Focus on the present shot as if you were on the first tee.

Pressure is playing for ten dollars when you don't have a dime in your pocket.
LEE TREVINO

Pressure is self defined and situational specific. What you feel as pressure on the golf course is very different from the pressure Tiger feels on the course. In life some people say they have high pressure jobs and golf is a getaway, while others have low pressure jobs, yet feel tremendous pressure on the golf course. Realize you are the one who defines if a situation creates pressure or not. Think back to when you first began playing golf. You experienced different pressures than you do now. Then it was the pressure of just getting the ball airborne, now it may be gambling with your friends. Dealing with pressure is two fold: (1) Define what pressure really is and put your game in perspective and (2) Realize that through experience of playing in different situations you have increased your comfort zone and have learned to deal with pressure better.

Modeling the best and understanding how they deal with pressure is very helpful. Think of a player you admire for his ability to deal with pressure. Modeling is basically copying how the best walk, talk, and carry themselves in these pressure-packed situations. Tiger Woods, to me, is the best at dealing with pressure situations. Tiger loves the competition and says his sense of focus gets better under pressure. Tiger defines pressure as something enjoyable, while many other top players define it as tough or grinding. Tiger looks forward to those situations where he can test himself internally. He is so sure of himself that pressure improves his performance. Ask some players you know how they deal with pressure. You may be surprised how simple it is to play your best when the stakes are high. By practicing how you think the best would handle pressure you start developing new behaviors and habits for yourself. Just like a golf swing needs practice; your skills dealing with pressure also need to be practiced.

Most sports psychology coaches will have the golfer practice his pre-shot routine as a way to combat the negative reaction to pressure. This may work for a few golfers, but you need to understand why pressure is affecting your game in a negative way.

Pressure is linked negatively to:

- Muscle tension

- Mind racing- poor decision making

- Poor self-talk

- Easy distraction

- Self doubt

Once you know how you personally handle pressure you can then improve. If muscle tension is the biggest problem then breathing techniques will be very beneficial. If you are distracted easily then focus drills like meditation can be useful. We are all different in how we perceive pressure and how we perform while feeling it. Throughout this book you will find other ways of turning pressure into an ally.

Remember that anxiety is a natural part of performing. Even champion golfers feel the butterflies before a big tournament. When you get anxious or excited your heart beats faster, you breathe faster, and your muscles tense. What you do with this anxiety is the key. If your focus goes to how stressed out you are then it becomes a distraction in executing the present shot.

Centering is a technique that is used to break the negative feedback loop and gain back physical control of your body. Centering utilizes deep breathing and the sensation of grounding your body. Taking a deep breath and feeling your feet becoming rooted to the ground will remind you of staying present. By consciously doing the breathing and being aware of your feet you change from negative outcome thinking to process thinking. The process thinking is what steps I need to take to perform at my best. These processes will break the downward spiral of negative anxiety.

Another technique is to replay an old performance problem that was caused by anxiety and see yourself using breathing and centering to regain control. Play the scenario out with this new understanding of controlling your anxiety by getting centered. You will have confidence the next time you are feeling anxiety that you can regain control because of the positive visualizations.

The emotional state that you are in will directly affect how you perform. Learn which emotional state serves you the best and concentrate on ways to reconnect with that state when you are off. You need to be in control, don't let golf control you. Be that emotional state on and off the course so you can own it.

YOUR SHOT

- Identify your best arousal state to play great golf

- What is your anchor that you will use to get into your peak emotional state?

- Identify what gets you out of that optimal performance state

- Take the bad results as a challenge and stay in the game mentally

- Which tool will you use to maintain and regain your optimal performance state?

- Which emotions do you want to experience on the course?

- Which emotions don't you want to experience on the course?

(6)

PLANNING TO BE GREAT/ PREPARATION

WHAT YOU WILL LEARN:

- How To Practice To Reach Your Goals

- How To Prepare For A Round

- How To Be Ready For A Tournament

- How To Think Before A Shot

Most golfers prepare for disaster. A good golfer prepares for success.
BOB TOSKI

I try to simulate the most difficult conditions
the players will encounter during competition.
MIKE HOLDER, former golf coach for Oklahoma State

chapter

6

Very often golfers just show up to the golf course without thinking about what their plan is for that round. Planning is about preparation. Plan to succeed by looking at all facets of your game. How should you prepare yourself to give yourself the best chance to perform at your highest level? Every player does things they feel have helped them to perform well. When you develop a plan to improve your performance you will increase your confidence and play better on the course. Without a plan, plan on failing.

Planning provides:

• Clarity of tasks

• Feeling of certainty

• A way to uncover any potential obstacles

The harder I practice the luckier I get.
GARY PLAYER

WHAT TO PLAN FOR:

PRACTICE SESSIONS

What is the goal of practice? It should be to turn conscious motor skills into unconscious motor skills so you can play golf with a repeatable swing/stroke that produces consistently high performance results. Practice is definitely used to learn new skills or refine a certain move. This is the training part of practice that every athlete must continue to include in practice. Your goal of practice is to solidify your fundamentals and perfect the best swing for you. The best swing for you is based on your physical capabilities and the realistic time you can spend in making changes. Every golfer wants a better golf swing, but will not or cannot put in the proper amount of time to make the necessary changes. I have also seen golfers spend hours on the range per week with no purpose and looking like they are hitting balls just for the exercise.

The challenge in the past five to ten years is the information overload that golfers experience through new technology, books, magazines, and The Golf Channel. Golfers are getting more confused every time they open the latest golf magazine that reveals the five secrets to straighten out your slice. However, well meaning, these tips might contradict the tips from the previous month's edition. The golfer reads the article, goes to the range to try out the tip and gets frustrated that the tip doesn't work. The other problem is the amazing new technology that is out there for golf instructors to use to help their students. I have personally used video cameras, dynamic balance machines, body motion jackets, and launch monitors. All of these aids have great benefit to the teacher; however, when the teacher and student rely too much on statistics and not on the end result of better play then there is a problem. If we can't get out of our analytical mind to make a swing then we lose the creative side of what makes golf fun. The balance is a tricky one, yet you must give yourself time during practice to be both analytical and creative.

I encourage golfers to foster their creativity on the practice range. Experiment hitting different shots: high, low, fade, draw, etc. When you allow yourself to try different shots, you begin to push out of your comfort zone. You will now feel like you have more shots at your disposal. These options will be mastered when you spend some of your time working on them. I like experimenting because it allows a golfer to get out of having to do things only one way. Seeing there are different possibilities can get a golfer out of an analyzing mindset and shifting to a creative mindset. Golfers while experimenting with different shots have a lot more fun practicing. Pulling off a shot that once seemed impossible is a great feeling. When you practice these shots more you can take them on the golf course and save strokes.

Practice time is all about the process goals that you mapped out in chapter three. Use this time to work on the skills that are needed to boost your performance and get closer to your outcome goals. Take the few minutes before a practice session to be clear on what you want to accomplish and how you will accomplish it. Just saying you want to improve your swing by hitting seven irons will do very little to improve your performance level. Become specific. For example, a practice goal might be to straighten out the direction of your driver. The how would be the specific drills that your instructor gave you to learn a new plane. You might also review your pre-shot fundamentals such as grip, alignment, and posture which have the most impact on your swing. Be focused on each swing to insure you are getting the most out of your practice. By being focused you are also helping the skill of focus that is needed while you play.

Developing the skills needed to improve your golf game comes down to prioritizing what you will spend your time on practicing. Many golfers fall into the, "I don't have enough time to practice everything so I will just reinforce what I am doing well." This is classified as the muscle memory idea of repetition of already learned skills. This player doesn't make any huge jump in overall performance. People love to do what they are good at, it makes us feel good inside and keeps our confidence high. The true champions of any sport are those athletes who work on their weaknesses and bring these areas up to the level of the areas that are already strong. This is about being honest with yourself and knowing that if you work on your weaknesses your entire game will get better. On the course we often play to avoid our weaknesses. I used to be a poor wedge player from 60-90 yards, so I would do whatever I could to avoid having those shots on the course. This was a game that was defensive and fearful of being in that yardage range. It wasn't until I spent a month refining my wedge game that I knew I could hit those shots. I was stubborn and didn't like working on my weaknesses. So my game never reached a higher level until I made my weaknesses a priority in my practice.

Go back to chapter three on goal setting and review the section on performance and process goals. In order for your outcome goals to be accomplished, you need to improve your performance goals through better practicing habits. What level of performance does each part of your game need to be at in order to accomplish your ultimate goal? When you realize that you're up and down percentage needs to improve you can schedule the time in your practice. Action needs to be taken to improve skills and to get the most out of your practice. You must prioritize your practice time.

Another part of prioritizing is practicing the shots you play the most in an actual round. How often have you practiced on the range by hitting just seven irons to groove your swing? This is acceptable in the training mindset; however, to practice the trusting mindset you need to practice with all your clubs. If time is a concern concentrate on the big three: the driver, wedge, and putter. You hit a majority of your shots with these three clubs, so it makes sense to use our practice time mastering these vital clubs.

I have mentioned that practice is both training new skills and allowing the new skills to become automatic. Your time needs to be split between training a skill and trusting a skill. The training part is the typical hit balls and "work on the swing." The problem with staying in the training mode is you are never testing to see if it will hold up on the golf course. You need to test the skills by simulating course situations. This is the trusting mindset. Take time out to the practice session to hit golf shots, not golf swings. This requires you to aim at a target, pick a club, and commit to a shot. To take this a step further, compete with a friend on the practice range or putting green. The competition will create similar feelings you experience on the course. You are now testing your skills to see if they are automatic. I used to play a game of "Horse" with my friends when I practiced. We would call shots out and see who could pull the shot off. The loser would buy lunch. What this game pushed me to do was get out of my analytical mode and into a creative mode. We would hit crazy shots like fifty yards hooks with eight irons or seventy yards slices with a driver. By creating you learn to let go of perfect mechanics. You will also learn a lot about cause and effect and be able to play trouble shots better and know why regular swings are creating poor results.

Practicing your short game is no different. Prioritize your time with working on weaknesses, skill development, and creativity. Short game has always been underestimated for how important it is to your score. Commit to take time to improve shots within 100 yards. When I was an instructor, students asked for short game lessons very rarely, yet when I forced them to take a couple they saw immediate improvement. Take a lesson, practice the skills, and practice under pressure.

One of my favorite drills to teach focus and trusting is done on the putting green. Many top professionals have said they include a variation of this drill in their practice sessions. It has to do with having a goal of making a predetermined number of putts in a row. Each session you would increase the number to continue to push yourself. Go to the practice putting green. Start with putts of three feet. Set the goal of making twenty in a row before you leave the putting green. This drill is not all about making a three-foot putt, it is about how you think and perform when you have made seventeen, eighteen, or nineteen in a row. Where do your thoughts go? Can you stay focused on the present putt and trust your mechanics. If you feel pressure on the last few putts that is a sign that this practice is working because you can now simulate what it would be like to have to make a three foot putt on the eighteenth hole to shoot your career low round. Practice under the same pressure you experience on the golf course and you will perform better when you are on the course.

Where you practice can affect the quality of your practice time. I always enjoy practicing at the far end of the practice range. I did this so I would not be distracted by watching other players and it helped me stay focused on my session. For me that far stall on the right signified my office. When I was in my office it was time to practice with a purpose. I see so many golfers at a practice range who get distracted by watching what other players are doing, they start to change what they intended to work on in the first place.

Sometimes the best practice is that done in the off season. In some parts of the country it is not realistic to play or practice during the winter months. Utilize this time to work on the fundamentals of the swing. You can grip a club everyday, so you maintain the feel. New training devices such as heavy clubs are useful to keep your golf muscles active.

This downtime can be very beneficial to work on your mental game. Use the time you would usually play golf by visualizing your swing. By visualizing your perfect swing you can make improvements at a faster rate than if you just swung a club. Visualize the attainment of your golf goals for the next season and map out the plan for what skills need to be improved. Look back at the last golf season and evaluate your progress and what you learned. All of these visualizations will provide motivation when the season starts.

Use different learning strategies to make improvements. By utilizing mirrors, training devices and a heavy club you will be able to see and feel your swing in different ways. I have had my biggest swing discoveries at home in front of a mirror when I was trying to implement a change in my swing. Take these experiences into your visualization to solidify the mind/body connection. At home you can work on your putting by checking fundamentals of grip, stance, and alignment. Using a metronome can improve your tempo for both your putting and golf swing. Just like outside practice work both on skill development and being creative.

ROUND- BE READY TO PLAY

The following is taken from *Psyching for Sport: Mental Training for Athletes,* by Terry Orlick, Human Kinetics Publishers, 1986

The goal of preparation is to help you attain the ideal state for performance. The following questions are designed to help you identify how you need to think and feel in order to perform at your best.

Think of your **best** performance in the past year and respond to the following:

1. How did you feel just before the event?

2. What were you saying to yourself or thinking before the start of the event?

3. How were you focused during the event? What were you aware of or paying attention to during the event?

Now think of you **worst** performance in the past year when responding to the following?

1. How did you feel before the event?

2. What were you saying to yourself or thinking before the start of the event?

3. How were you focused during the event? What were you aware of or paying attention to during the event?

4. What were the major differences in your energy level and your thoughts prior to these two performances? In your focus of attention during the performance?

5. How would you prefer to think/feel prior to a competitive performance? How would you prefer to focus during the competition?

This was one of the first assignments I had to fill out in my first Sports Psychology class. I learned that my performances were far more about my mental and emotional state then how my swing was performing. These responses can be used to guide you in the development of a mental and physical routine before an important round. You can take control by purposely directing your thoughts, images, and focus. Use what has been successful for you in the past. Develop a routine that incorporates constructive self-talk, images, and attentional focus. Self-talk before a round should be positive, motivating, and simple. Using cue words will accomplish those aspects of self-talk. Repeating words like "focus", "I've done it before", and "stay in the present" are all examples of good cue words and can be used before and during a round. Your mental images should recall past successes or future successes. This will boost your confidence and help you develop a strategy.

Having process goals for the round is also important. These are the actions that are under your control and will have a direct effect on your outcome. What do you want to accomplish in this round? A process goal would be to commit fully to each image that day or regulate your emotional state.

When planning for a round it is important to realize what your ability level is and is not. I encourage my students to create a personal par for each hole. This allows a golfer to minimize high scores and deal with bogeys in a more positive manner. For instance, an eighteen handicap who hits a driver 230 yards will have difficulty making a par on a 450 yard par 4. When this happens, a golfer will press to hit two perfect shots. Unfortunately, both the drive and second shot are poor, then the golfer tries to play catch up on the hole and makes a double bogey or worse. If the same golfer viewed this hole as a personal par of 5 it takes the pressure off of hitting "perfect" shots and bogey becomes very realistic and bigger scores are avoided. Personal par will help you plan your rounds more effectively. You will know when it would be best to hit three wood off the tee or lay-up on demanding par 4s.

To play your best golf you should prepare the night before. I keep a ritual that helps me get prepared for the next days round. I start by cleaning my clubs and shoes. I like having my equipment in the best shape possible before a round. I then inventory my bag to see if I have enough balls, tees, divot repair tool, rule book, sunscreen, band aids, and any other miscellaneous items that I may need. I stock the bag with snacks such as almonds and protein bars. If I have played the course before I will find an old scorecard or yardage book from that course and review it. This helps me reacquaint myself with the types of holes and shots that I need to play. I will then visualize the round of golf. Going through the entire round shot for shot. I am visualizing success with every shot and seeing myself handle the round by having fun. This visualization sets the tone for the next day's event.

Preparing for a round requires warming up both body and mind. Certain steps will help you be ready to play your best.

1. Get plenty of sleep the night before.

2. Eat a light meal at least ninety minutes before you tee off.

3. Give yourself plenty of time to arrive at the golf course. Don't feel rushed getting to the first tee. Rushing the last minute has ruined many a game!

4. Stretch before swinging the club. Basic stretches will do a lot in preparing the body for the round ahead.

5. Hit balls on the range and focus on target awareness and warming up the body. Many golfers make the mistake of hitting balls before the round as a practice session and try to fix their swing. Use this time to develop the tempo and balance that will help you play your best. Keep your swing thoughts to a minimum.

6. Keep your warm up to just thirty to fifty balls. Going over that limit might cause fatigue later in the round.

7. Warm-up short game. Hit chips, pitches, bunker, and putts before the round to acclimate yourself to how the greens are responding. You want to hit these types of shots to lock in your feel, so you know you can get up and down when necessary.

"Play with better players" is advice I heard as a junior golfer and it helped me learn faster on what it takes to play at a higher level. I would watch these better players how they reacted after poor shots, how they executed certain shots, and how they prepared before important rounds. After a round invite one of these players to lunch and pick their brain on how they got to the level they are at now. This technique is called modeling. Find someone who has accomplished what you want to achieve and find out how they did it. Once you know their "recipe for success" you can copy it. Learning from better players will reduce your learning curve and get you to your golfing goals sooner.

TOURNAMENT- KNOW WHAT YOU NEED TO DO

Preparing for a tournament round is very similar to any other round of golf. There are a few differences that I advocate you take to maximize your chances for peak performance. The biggest change to Phil Mickelson's golf game from 2004 and on has been his improvement of preparation before a major championship. He visits the site of each major sometimes months in advance to scout out a game plan. His focus, with the help of instructor Dave Pelz, is to understand the percentages of which short game shots are the best to play in certain areas around the green. This does two important things: (1) He is more confident in choosing the correct shot and (2) The preparation allows him to lay-up when he is in trouble to spots he knows he has a great chance to get up and down. The proof this form of preparation is in his performance in majors after 2004. He finally broke through to capture his first win and shortly followed with two more wins.

In Analyzing his game, his preparation won it for him. His swing hadn't improved measurably the past three years, but his preparation allowed him to make better decisions around the green. However, as we saw on the seventy-second hole at the 2006 U.S. Open Phil deviated from the plan and reverted back to his aggressive nature and did not play the percentages costing him the U.S. Open.

- Play a practice round: understand where you don't want to leave yourself. For example, some holes are designed to entice you to play aggressively when playing to the front edge of a green is the best shot. Use the practice round as a way to develop a plan.

- Prepare for slow play- 90% of the time tournament golf means slow golf. Many players hate slow play and it definitely affects how they play in a tournament. The first thing is to assume there will be slow play and instill the idea of patience as you get to the golf course. Have a plan for slow play. I encourage my clients to focus on non-golf topics between shots or when there is a long wait before the next shot. Give your mind a break and then have a trigger to get you back to the present shot. A pre-shot routine may work, yet for slow play I even like to add another reminder to switch my focus back to the present shot. It might be the trigger of putting your glove on your hand. This signals you that the wait is over and it is time to be focused on the shot.

- Prepare what shots are needed- Every course possesses unique challenges. Maybe there are long par-3's that require long irons. Preparing the week before the tournament practice those shots you may not play all the time.

It has been written that Tiger Woods gets the pin sheet before a round and then practices in his warm-up routine. This gives him the opportunity to hit different shots and make the best decision once he gets on the golf course. You may not have that information, however, you can think ahead to where some of the hole location will be and plan accordingly.

One of the best pieces of advice that I have heard came from Ben Hogan He is quoted as saying that one of the first things he did to prepare for an US Open tournament was to walk the course backwards. This helped him see the best places to come in from on approach shots and where he could miss it around the greens. We may not have that luxury before a tournament; however, it is a good idea that once you play a hole during a practice round to look from the green back toward the tee. Your perspective will be different and could cause you to change a game plan for the next time you play that hole. Be in a mindset of learning so your preparation will get better and better. The more you properly prepare the odds are the more confident you will be when you step up to the first tee.

As you approach a tournament I suggest playing more and practicing less. This will get you more in the trusting mindset rather than getting stuck in the training mindset. You want to pace yourself both physically and mentally. Do not practice and play excessively more than you have in the past. Being prepared is about doing what is necessary to be ready, but still having enough gas in the tank to do it. I see many who practice more than they can handle and are burned out when the tournament begins.

If you are going to play in a multiple day tournament you will face different challenges than playing in a one day format. The preparation should include how you will spend your time between rounds. Some like to get as far away from thinking about golf as possible. They go to the movies, another sporting event, or a show. This helps them take their minds off the day's rounds and minimizes thinking ahead to the upcoming rounds. Some golfers stay in golf mode. They practice heavily after a tournament round. Even at home or the hotel room they think about the round they played and the next day's strategy. Experience will tell you what would work best. A tournament that has more than one round can be challenging especially for those who are near the lead for the first time. Their mind races to the "what ifs" of winning. They think about it so much that it burns them out mentally and creates more emotional anxiety.

There is an ideal route for every hole ever built.
The more precisely you can identify it, the greater your chances for success.
JACK NICKLAUS

THE ACTUAL SHOT- PREPARE FOR TAKE-OFF

- Pre-shot routine- prepare your mind and body to execute at your best

- Physical routine

- Mental routine

The goal of the pre-shot routine is to get you physically, mentally, and emotionally ready to be able to commit to the present golf shot. The physical part to the routine might include a practice swing, body scan to evaluate tension level, and how you align yourself. Your routine is individual to you. You don't have to copy someone else's routine. Find out what works for you. For instance many players I work with take additional practice swings on short game shots compared to full swings. A practice swing serves the purpose of feeling the shot before you execute. Use the physical part of the routine to get yourself in the correct arousal state to execute the shot.

Planning takes very little energy, yet has profound results. Being prepared will boost your confidence, improve decision making, and allow you to execute more freely then ever before. If you want to become a better player, then you must learn how to prepare. Planning to hit your shot leads you to execution of the shot. The next chapter will go in depth on what to think before a shot and what gets in the way of performing your best.

YOUR SHOT

- When you played your best, how did you prepare?

- Try out a pre-round routine that gets you warmed up physically, mentally focused, and emotionally ready

- Plan a strategy for an upcoming golf round

EXECUTION-
YOUR ABILITY TO FOCUS

WHAT YOU WILL LEARN:

- How To Block Out Distractions

- How To Commit To Shots

- The Ability To Execute Under Pressure

A lot of us are good but Jack Nicklaus adds one intangible.
I think he knows exactly what his capabilities are in any given situation.
We may think we can pull off a shot, or even be pretty sure, but Jack knows.
RAYMOND FLOYD

Seve's a rare kind of guy. He's an excitable golfer who can concentrate.
LARRY NELSON- on Seve Ballesteros

I couldn't care less who I am paired with.
JACK NICKLAUS

To me the gallery becomes nothing but a wall. I don't even see faces.
LANNY WADKINS

chapter

7

Visualize your shot first. Then trust the images you see,
trust the mechanics that you've practiced, and simply be a shot maker.
WALLY ARMSTRONG, golf Instructor

The more I focus, the less I worry about pressure.
NICK PRICE

The one skill that separates the great professionals from the average player is the ability to focus. Peak performance requires that you execute while being fully engaged in the task at hand. The difference between playing your best and playing inconsistently has to do with the ability to switch from the training mindset to the trusting mindset. When we practice we are usually in the training mindset of learning and developing our skills. The best are able to let go from the learning mindset and embrace the trusting mindset. The trusting mindset is where we can just play and let go. Too many golfers experience playing well in practice and not playing as well in the actual round. The issue revolves around focus and pressure. On the course these golfers have a difficult time focusing on the process and get stuck in either the outcome or the mechanics of the shot. Also, the golfer feels the pressure change his arousal level that in turn makes him feel uncomfortable. This pressure creates tension in the body and affects the decision making of the golfer.

I joke with my clients that on the range we hit shots that we don't have to find. We hit shot after shot that doesn't result in a consequence to our score. This allows us to relax and just hit shots. If we don't like the result we get to immediately try again and it didn't cost us a penalty shot. On the course the golfer begins to fear the poor shot which creates the tension in the body.

This tension is not felt on the range during practice, so the golfer is trying to execute the same shot, but with a different physical state. The goal of practice is to make our skills unconscious so we can just play. Unfortunately tension changes our ability to swing the same. Once a golfer steps on the first tee his expectations and perceptions change from the practice range. The golfer perceives more pressure to perform which creates a different emotional state.

We have already addressed the importance of finding your best emotional state. If you are too excited you may begin to play too quickly and make poor decisions. Pressure is self inflicted. What is pressure for you is different for another golfer. Some excel in the pressure situation because they have defined pressure as a good thing. The champions use pressure as a motivator, while others see pressure as a threat. Others see pressure as another opportunity to screw up and embarrass themselves. How do you define pressure? The self talk you use to define the moment will affect your physical and emotional state. Do you say things like: "It's do or die, it's now or never, no tomorrow" or "This is going to be fun, this is why I practice, I love the challenge." Just saying those phrases will affect how your physical and emotional parts will respond. The easiest way to change your response to pressure is by defining it differently. Change the words you use to get yourself ready to play.

The skill of focus will help you execute at the highest level. Execution in golf basically means taking action toward a goal or toward a golf shot. The ability to take decisive action is what separates the champions from the rest.

Focus has two components:

1. Knowing what to do

2. Being able to stay present while doing it

The skill of focus requires you to go through the 4 focus channels. The focus channel technique was developed by Dr. Robert Nideffer.

	{Awareness}		{Execute}
1.	Broad/External	4.	Narrow/External
2.	Broad/Internal	3.	Narrow/Internal
	{Analyze}		{Planning, Rehearse}

We all have our preferences that we will use too much when under pressure. For instance I analyze too much when I feel pressure. This gets in the way of me moving through my focus channels and ultimately executing with my entire focus. When we experience strong emotions such as anger, doubt, or frustration this breaks down our ability to shift between different focus channels.

GOLF SPECIFIC 4 FOCUS CHANNELS

Step One- Broad/External. Take in your environment. Become aware of yardage, weather, hole location, lie of shot, etc.

Step Two- Broad/Internal. Analyze what all this information means to you and your skill set. Start deciding on target, club selection, and type of shot

Step Three- Narrow/Internal. Plan the shot out, rehearse. Take a practice swing. Does it feel right? Narrow all the possibilities down to one.

Step Four- Narrow, External. Execute, turn focus to target and let go.

Many golf instructors teach their students to lag putt on long putts. They advocate visualizing hitting within a three foot circle. This to me is a disservice. I understand the reasoning behind it; however you are now programming yourself to miss the putt. Sure the percentages are lower on longer putts, but the goal of golf is to get the ball in the hole in as few shots as possible. Your mind likes to have as specific a target as possible to shoot for. If you miss the three foot circle by an inch you would still have a 3 foot putt, if you miss the hole by an inch, you now have a one inch putt. What is the outcome of the shot you want specifically, not generally? An example that seems positive, yet can be detrimental is when we tell ourselves that "all I need is a two putt here to win the match." You're telling yourself that missing the first putt is fine and this creates a general focus instead of a narrow focus toward making the putt.

DISTRACTIONS

Focusing seems so easy when we have steps to follow. However you know maintaining your proper focus on the golf course is challenging. What gets in the way of focus? Distractions take you out of your focus channels. What are your distractions?

Common distractions are:

- Playing partners

- Slow play

- People watching

- Internal doubt

- Fear of failure

- Hazards

- Sounds

- Personal Issues

- Swing thoughts

- A hole played poorly in the past

- Comparing your score to others

Distractions get in the way of the ability to completely stay in the moment. If our mind is not focused on the process of executing the best shot, you will then produce inconsistent results. You need to analyze what gets you out of executing with complete commitment. Your distractions are different than others. You may be distracted by noise, movement, or internal chatter. Analyze past issues with focus so you can change how you deal with these distractions in a positive way.

The time between shots in golf can be an asset or liability depending on what you focus on. As you go between shots you could focus on the result of the last shot (good or bad), you could focus on the next shot (result and process), or you could focus on what you are going to have for dinner after the round. You control where you place your attention. It is acceptable if you thought of all three of the above things as long as you didn't allow them to get in the way of your commitment on the shot. It is natural to think of the last shot or future shots. When we use this time to regain focus by taking deep breaths or thinking of non-golf items we can reenergize ourselves between shots. Some use the time between shots to create fear, while other use it as a pep talk to boost confidence.

Identify are these external distractions such as noise or are they internal such as our mindset. See if any of these distractions are under your control.

If so, do something about it. If not, go with the flow and learn to refocus attention on the moment.

Ways to improve execution focus:

1. Meditation

2. Neurofeedback

3. Breathing

4. Attention to a small object- like the dimple on a ball

Meditation can improve performance in as little as 10 minutes a day. Find a place where you can be free from distractions. Choose a simple word like calm, smooth, relax to repeat to yourself mentally. Sit in an upright position, close your eyes, and repeat your word mentally over and over. If your mind wanders bring attention back to breath and your word. By practicing this you will improve focusing skills, regulate body tension better, and develop an inner calm that will serve you well on the golf course.

I use a machine called The Peak Achievement Trainer that is a neurofeedback device that trains the student to narrow his focus. The device connects to a computer and the student is instructed to focus on parts of the screen. Instantly the student sees if his focus is narrowing or getting distracted. This use of new technology is readily available and has been helping world champion athletes for years.

The use of breath is the simplest of ways to improve your focus. With attention to breathing you will instantly find yourself slowing down and narrowing focus. Start by being aware of the breath going in your nose, hold for a couple of counts, and release the breath through your mouth slowly. As you work on this simple technique you can experiment with alternate breathing patterns that can benefit your focus.

Since the last step of the focus channel routine is on a narrow object, it makes sense to practice keeping your focus on a narrow object. My favorite is to stare at a golf ball and then fixate on one dimple. I stay absorbed with the dimple and remain focused on it. When my focus is distracted from the dimple I notice the distraction and then immediately bring my attention back to the dimple. Just taking 5 minutes a day on this one exercise will teach you to narrow your focus and deal with distractions a lot more effectively.

As the last quadrant of the focus channels indicates you need to be focused on something external to allow yourself to fully execute the shot. Research has proven time and time again that athletes who are focused internally on their performance either their technique or their mental state perform poorly compared to those who put their focus on a target. When focus stays internal the mind tends to race which disconnects the golfer from the ultimate outcome. A more productive way to execute is to focus on how you want the shot to come off, its trajectory, shape, and distance and turn it over to the body to execute. When I was playing competitive golf I would practice a drill that helped me just let go. I would hit balls on the range and have my friend call out a shot (fade, draw, or straight) in the middle of my backswing. I would have to create the shot at the top of the swing and on the downswing. What it did was help me think of the outcome and let my body respond. I wasn't locked into being perfect with mechanics; I began to trust that I could produce a shot literally in the middle of a swing. Another great drill is to look at the hole while you putt. With your eyes at the target you just respond with your arms and putter. You will be amazed how good you putt when you are locked into a target with no internal focus.

The ego gets in the way of performance as it can cloud your judgment of what is the correct shot to play in the moment. Those who play with their ego are those who are worried about how they measure up to others. The ego tells the golfer to take risks, to try and hit the ball further. Many times when I played junior and college golf I wanted to be the long ball hitter. I would make sure that no one was hitting a club to a par 3 that was less than me. If everyone was hitting a 9 iron on a 150 yard hole, I would also choose a 9 iron. Now I could only hit the 9 iron 140 yards. You can see what the result was, short in the bunker. It sounds ridiculous, however many of my decisions on the golf course were ego driven. Check your ego at home. Know your skill level and make decisions based on that level, not fantasy skills. Only play shots that you have practiced. Confidence in a particular shot you want to hit will be related to how often you have successfully hit this shot in practice.

Playing from trouble or awkward lies takes a different mindset. As a rule these shots have not been practiced enough to give you a definite knowledge of what will happen. This doubt creates confusion in the golfer and disaster then ensues. Trouble shots require a clear understanding of risk vs. reward based on your skill level. Playing the percentages is crucial when you are experiencing a shot that you feel uneasy about. Visualizing different ways the shot might go will lead to visualizing the shot that you can actually attempt to pull off. Understanding basics of ball flight from different lies and slopes will give you a better chance of making a correct decision. For example if the ball is a foot above your feet at setup you need to know that the tendency is for the ball to hook (right handed golfer) to the left off of the slope. The goal is make an educated guess so you are committed to a decision.

Playing your game on the golf course is vital for long-term success. Too many get caught up playing a game that doesn't fit their real strengths and they are forced to play a game they do not possess. Sure, I would love to over-power a course like Tiger, but I don't possess that skill. When you check your game based on reality, instead of a distorted perception you will find you will play the game with more enjoyment and will have lower scores.

Knowing your game and playing your game consists of:

- Playing to your personality and your psychological and physical characteristics

- Realistically assessing the risk-and-reward factor of a shot and your capabilities

- Basing your game on your experience level, style of play, power, touch, and finesse

- Having the discipline to focus just on your game

- Understanding what you can and cannot control

- Employing your best tempo and pace of play

- Committing to your course strategy

The one distraction that I hear from all level of players is the golfer who thinks about his swing instead of thinking of the target. This distraction can be broken down into two sections:

1. Those who know what they want to accomplish and run all the "swing thoughts" through their mind. They have taken the lessons and know the "7 keys" for them that will result in a good shot.

2. Those who are always searching for a different swing. They don't like their swing and are on the hunt for the perfect swing. They change monthly depending on the articles in the latest edition of a golf magazine.

Both types will be constantly distracted on the golf course for the rest of their playing life. As I said before, the last part of execution is to turn your attention to the external target, not to stay in your head with a laundry list of swing thoughts. Prepare yourself the best you can before a round and during a shot. The skill of letting go and pulling the trigger is key. By having excessive swing thoughts you are trying to control the swing too much. This has the opposite effect; you don't allow your body to react to the target. Instead of having a list of words that you mentally check off, switch to images and feelings. Golf is a "feel" game, yet we try to play it intellectually with words that don't convey feel. A good swing image would be to imagine swinging your club on a tilted circle instead of thinking, don't forget to get the club in the 45 degree angle at the ¾ position with full set of wrists. Keep it simple so your mind can react to the target.

There comes a time in everyone's golf career when they embrace the swing they have. Don't get me wrong I want all my clients to seek professional instruction to refine and improve their skills. There is a fine balance between a golfer wanting a better swing and one who wants to play better golf. Having a better swing mechanically doesn't guarantee you will shoot lower scores. There are many great players on the tours who have "unique" swings who learned to own their swing and perfect their swing. These players include: Nancy Lopez, Jim Furyk, Lee Trevino, and Raymond Floyd. They have all won major championships and can play great golf with unorthodox swings.

The other type of golfer is always listening to what others say about their swing. They want to get better so they seek out a new swing guru to take them to the next level. More often then not this guru changes the very thing that made the players swing work, in favor of a more "mechanically sound" swing. Now the player is relearning a swing that used to be second nature. Unfortunately, more times than not the result of the change is disastrous. This has happened to major championship winners Ian Baker Finch and Seve Ballesteros. The worst case scenario is when a feel player is forced to become a mechanical player. Would you change Fred Couples swing to look more like Nick Faldo's? No because what makes Couples' swing so successful is different than what makes Nick Faldo's swing successful. Most players already have their "swing DNA". They can make refinements, but to try to overhaul it would be counterproductive. To be the best, you have to search for your best swing, not the best swing.

Start understanding what makes your swing work, instead of always questioning why your swing doesn't work. Next time you take a lesson, ask your instructor why your swing works at times. Once you know that you can perfect those things. Instead, our tendency is to always ask our instructor why our swing doesn't work. You must believe in your swing. Those who believe in their method are better off than someone who has a "great swing" yet doesn't truly believe it.

Of all the hazards, fear is the worst.
SAM SNEAD

Fear is a human emotion that can stop us in our tracks from performing. The fears can include many things, yet the fear most experienced is the fear of failure. Fear of failure can start out as small insecurities and build to a belief system that makes it difficult to even take the club back. Sometimes fear of failure can be used to motivate an individual to work harder. In golf the fear of "losing my swing" becomes a driving force to practice even when one is playing well.

Past memories of a hole can affect our ability to commit to a shot. I hear it all the time about the one hole that the golfer always makes double bogey on and the golfer knows it is going to happen every time. There are holes that perhaps don't set up for your ball flight and visually look deceiving to you. You must be careful in the language you use when you step on the tee. Take the words "always" and "every time" out of your vocabulary. If you step up to the tee and say "I always screw up this hole", you are not leaving yourself any other options. Learn from what you did wrong on the hole and make adjustments. Don't dwell on the past outcomes or you will keep your focus on poor results and thus affect the current shot. Break the hole down from shot to shot. If it is a dogleg right par four with trouble all along the right side then think of how you will best play the first shot. This may mean a change in club or target from previous attempts. After you make a decision with what outcome target you want to hit, you must get into the process of giving yourself the best chance to make a committed swing. If a hole has given you problems you can change what you say about the hole, change the visualization of the shot, or change your strategy for the shot. Golfers get stuck in what doesn't work and are not inclined to make changes.

Fear of success works on a more subconscious level as well. I have seen this with many talented players who look like world beaters on the practice range, but haven't performed to that level on the golf course. Sometimes golfers fear how good they could be and the responsibilities that go along with playing at a high level. Think about this because as much as we all want to play better golf we also feel pressure to live up to our low score every time out. Feeling comfortable shooting low scores and winning tournaments is something many have to work through and start embracing. There are many others who love shooting low scores and don't feel additional pressure to repeat it every time out. Fear of success is related to your belief system. Some don't believe that they are good players even though everyone around them tells them how good they are. Competitive golfers have admitted to me that if they win people will expect them to win again and again. This creates pressure that these players don't want.

Nobody but you and your caddie care what you do out there,
and if your caddie is betting against you, he doesn't care either.
LEE TREVINO

Looking bad in front of others is another driving fear that stops golfers from executing to their potential. When a golfer's attention is on what other people think it takes away from what matters at the moment of execution. This fear usually revolves around missing short putts, first tee jitters, and playing with strangers. When you put more importance into what others think about you than what you think about yourself, then you have a problem. I tell my clients that your perception of what other people are thinking about your game is quite different than the reality. Other people are worried about their own game; they could care less about your performance. The only time people care about your performance is if they are competing against you or if you are playing too slow.

A major distraction with players either new to competition or those outside of their comfort zone is being intimidated by another player. Your attention goes to someone else's game and you become more aware of how your game might be perceived. You start making comparisons. I found this out when I gave playing lessons to my students. They were so worried about playing with me that they completely melted down. Their performance suffered because they just wanted to get out of my way. What is interesting is that round of golf was supposed to be about the student, not me. I was there to demonstrate some shots and see my student perform on the course. I have experienced feelings of intimidation myself. I would putt out too soon and make mistakes. I would make sure I was never in another player's way. I was letting another player control my game. I don't get intimated anymore, I will get excited to play with certain golfers, but I play my own game. Give yourself the respect you deserve on the course. Golfers know the difficulty of the game and are not going to judge you based on a couple of bad shots.

First tee jitters are something every golfer has experienced. The reason that the first tee creates an emotional reaction is twofold: 1. we want to impress those watching (or not to embarrass ourselves in front of others) and 2. The first shot has more expectations tied to it. With the former we look at a human need of wanting approval from others. The first tee is usually the shot where most people are present. We may have just met our group members and would love to show them we can play. However most of us get into the mindset of "don't mess this shot up" while all these people are watching. First off most people don't care about your shot. That might surprise you, but they are concerned about their own shot. Once you have hit no one is going to remember that shot, except you. This shot requires the same routine as the rest of your shots. You may have to be aware of your arousal level and do some deep slow breaths to calm down and get control over your emotional state. Using the anchoring technique can also change your emotional state from fear to confidence in seconds. Visualization gets you to stay in the present and takes your attention off the people watching. The other reason why the first shot is viewed to be so important is because golfers feel this one shot will lead to success or failure for the rest of the round. This added pressure always backfires and leads to an increase in the arousal level. Change your belief about the first shot and treat it like any other shot you will have that day. It is no more important than the second shot on the first hole. By treating each shot the same you will develop better consistency off the first tee. Remember the proper process will lead to the desired outcome. If you focus on the outcome first you will affect the process too much. Commit to staying with your present process.

A strategy that I encourage my clients to embrace is the idea of stepping on the tee box as if you own it. Creating the tee box as a place you want to be instead of something to fear is the switch that is needed to perform better. A confident golfer doesn't care who is watching. In fact these players love to hit in front of people as a way to "show off" their skills. When you actually look forward to playing in front of others, this is a great place to be. It is very important to have a trigger that tells you it is time to focus on the shot. That may mean when you set your bag next to your ball or when you put your glove on your hand. This trigger will help you switch your focus and it creates a signal to block out distractions. This trigger will shift focus to the present moment and start your pre-shot routine.

From a pre-shot routine perspective the ability to stay relaxed and focused on the target can become challenging. When golfers are nervous they tend to move faster, think faster, and make decisions faster than if they were calm and confident. That is why the first tee produces so many more poor shots than other shots during a round. The mental and emotional state changes both the mind and body to react in a way that the golfer is not accustomed to. This is a time to purposely slow down your routine and become aware of your body. Walking slower and taking deep breaths will help you tap into your best performance state.

Just like other times you feel nervous the important skill is to focus on the process of making a good swing. On the first tee most golfers stay outcome focused on the potential result of the shot which creates expectations and added pressure. The solution is to feel the tempo and balance of a good swing through the proper use of a practice swing. Feeling the proper practice swing can lead to confidence and relax the body.

The attitude of playing golf to win, rather than playing golf not to lose will also affect your execution of a shot. I see it with good players all the time; they get a lead and begin to play not to lose it. The tension in their body increases. This tension stops the club from fully releasing and causes a block to the right. The attitude gets interpreted by the mind as control the club, instead of just letting go. Controlling the club during impact is counter productive. When you play your best you don't consciously think of controlling the club, you just swing and the club takes care of it. Playing to win is the attitude of staying present and treating each shot the same with the intention of hitting a great shot. Playing not to lose is the intention of don't hit a bad shot! This affects confidence and our ability to close out rounds. The best want to keep going lower and lower.

Perfectionism and golf do not go well together. I played the first part of my golfing career striving to be perfect. This standard can never be met and it led to self worth issues for me and I have seen in others. My first experience with golf was exciting and I remember looking at this little white ball and thinking how easy this game should be. I continued to play always thinking there must be a secret to the game that nobody has yet discovered. I continued my search. I would change clubs, change swings, change anything that I felt could get me closer to perfecting the game of golf. This was a rough time for me in my development. I would see other players with old clubs and self taught swings go out and have fun shooting lower scores than I was posting. Yet, I still moved on to be perfect. This attitude affected every shot I hit. I put undo pressure on myself and continued to compare my shots with what would be a perfect shot. This led to frustration and anger on and off the course. A game that looked so easy was turning into a game that was tearing me up inside.

I had to make a choice; should I continue down this road of frustration in hopes of finding the Holy Grail of golf or should I change my outlook and enjoy the journey? Luckily for me I had some great people around me who helped me see what I was doing to myself. I began to change my attitude towards the game. I now looked for ways to be excellent at golf instead of perfect. I still set high standards for my game; however I began to embrace my own skills, talents, and ways of playing. I looked to refine my game, not re-invent it every six months. Being perfect on the golf course is impossible, yet being excellent is possible. Reconnect with why you play golf. If it becomes just a game to try and perfect, be careful. If you play because you enjoy the challenge of testing your skills that's great; you will have a positive attitude toward the game.

Sometimes distractions have nothing to do with our golf. Thinking about personal issues and having these issues take up your attention is another way of causing execution problems. It is a skill to deal with personal problems off the golf course and keep your focus on the game. Write down what is bothering you and make time after the round to think and deal with these concerns. Remember where you place your attention; your action will follow. If your attention is on issues going on in your head then you will get stuck there and find it very difficult to be absorbed in your golf game. Part of a pre-round routine is finding something that transitions you to the role of a golfer and leaving the personal issues at home. I like the idea of writing down what is bothering you and leaving it on a table at home, knowing that you will deal with this 'stuff' after the round. The golf course is to play golf; home is the rest of your life. After the round you switch roles and do what needs to be done to handle your issues. You have to set up your golf time in a selfish way. We are all lucky to be able to play this great game and it can serve us in letting us get away from it all. Allow yourself to just play golf.

Our ability to focus and execute can change during a round for several reasons. Two reasons are mental and physical fatigue. When we get tired mentally it affects our arousal level and then the ability to focus. Golfers explain they get mentally "fried" during a round and find they make dumb mistakes at the end of a round. Mental fatigue shows up as impatience and reduced ability to focus.

Sources of mental fatigue:

- Playing too many days in a row

- Playing too many tournaments in a row

- Lack of balance in life- no time outside of golf

- Personal problems

Mental fatigue can be related to physical fatigue. When our body is tired it makes it more challenging for the mind to stay focused. We start focusing on how tired we feel and this takes away from being fully engaged in playing. The importance of physical fitness is a key to peak performance. Just improving your cardiovascular conditioning will help on a long day on the course. When you are as fresh on the 18th tee as you were on the 1st tee you will build confidence that you can finish strong.

VISUALIZATION/IMAGERY

Before every shot I go to the movies inside my head. Here's what I see.
First, I see the ball where I want it to finish in a specific small area
or fairway or green. Next I see the ball going there—its path, trajectory,
and behavior on landing. Finally, I see myself making the kind of swing
that will turn the first two images into reality. These home movies are a key
to my concentration and to my positive approach to every shot.
JACK NICKLAUS

The technique of visualization is one of the simplest and most powerful tools you have at your disposal. Visualization is used so many ways to improve performance:

- See a shot before you play it- provides confidence and clarity of type of shot

- Play an entire round of golf in your head as a mental practice round- this helps solidify a game plan and develops alternate ways of playing holes

- See yourself dealing with obstacles on the course- how do you want to act

- See yourself succeeding and achieving your goals- provides motivation and builds confidence

- See yourself making great golf swings- helps in learning new skills and builds confidence

Visualization helps motivate, manage energy, boost confidence, perfect skills, refocus, and prepare for competition. Visualization can be used in many different areas to bolster your performance. Let's go in more detail on why visualization works and how to achieve it. Visualization is a form of mental rehearsal which allows you to experience and reinforce your best swing mechanics. Even more powerful is turning your visualization into detailed imagery. Now all senses, not just what you see is brought to your mental practice. As you imagine something, tap into how you would be feeling, what you would be saying, thinking, and even smelling. When you can create an image with all your senses it will make it seem real.

Visualization is classified as disassociated or associated. Disassociated visualization is when you imagine seeing yourself in a scene like watching yourself on a movie screen. Associated visualization is when you imagine that you are actually in the scene experiencing the environment. Both can help your performance. Seeing yourself performing a great swing will help learning a skill; while visualizing as if seeing out your eyes handling the pressure of a situation make it seem even more real.

Get creative in your visualization exercise. Change from color to black and white. Slow the experience down or speed it up. When you practice and can control how you visualize you are ready to take this on the course. The more precise you can be in your visualization the more powerful the results. Think about these questions to make your visualization even more powerful.

- How is your body positioned for the golf swing? How do various parts of your body feel? In what muscles do you feel tension/stress?

- Are you concentrating on the feeling of the golf swing? Include any cue words that would describe this feeling, such as "slow and smooth".

- What do you see while preparing for a shot? Where are your eyes focused? What do you see as you get ready to execute?

Every golfer has visualized in putting. We read a putt and what we are doing is visualizing the line. Some can visualize the entire role of the putt, while others just see parts of the putt. A great way to learn visualization on the green is to putt in the early morning on wet greens. As you putt watch the ball create a line through the morning dew. You will start to see the entire line a lot better. Take this on the course by seeing the "dew" line before you stroke the putt. See how close you were to the actual putt and continue to practice in this manner. Then when you have dry conditions you'll still see the line as if there was water on the green. The goal is to be able to see as detailed a line as possible so your mind and body are clear on what needs to happen. We have all experienced a time when we hit a putt and had two conflicting reads in our mind. The result was a weak, uncommitted stroke that didn't come close to the hole. Clear visualization will lead to better feel. With a specific target, seeing how you will get to the target takes away doubt. When you trust your line, your feel will follow.

There are ways not to use visualization. Unfortunately we use visualization the wrong way even though we don't realize it. The most common way visualization is used incorrectly is on shots over water. Most golfers will tell me that they don't want to go in the water. That's the obvious part. However when a golfer continues to dwell on the water they are programming the mind to take action toward the water. The golfer never gets off of what they don't want, the water, and get on to what they want which is the green. The water unfortunately becomes the target. The mind doesn't register the word 'not'. If I say to myself, "I do not want to go in the water." The mind has to first process the image of water before it negates it. As your focus stays on the very thing that you want to avoid, your actions will try to support the image in your mind. Be careful with the last image that is in your mind before you take the club back.

Quick ways to get focused:

- Close your eyes- block out visual distractions

- Take slow, deep, diaphragmatic breathes, bring attention to body

Practicing visualization can be a creative process. I encourage my clients to play with how they visualize. On the course this might be visualizing the hole as big as a basketball hoop. By enlarging size of the hole you will affect your level of confidence. Same goes with the clarity of your visualization.

Pretend you have a focus lens that you can adjust to make your visualization fuzzy or crystal clear. You have control over the quality of your image. With practice you will be able to change the size, shape, color, clarity, and speed of your visualization. Speed visualization is an advanced skill of visualization. Many golfers visualize a direct line of a ball flight that has a constant speed. In putting the ball starts out accelerating, then the speed plateaus in the middle of the putt and finally the ball slows down at the end of the putt. When you can match the speed of the ball in your visualization with what is actually happening you will find that you will be much more confident of your shot. Practicing with the speed of the ball will get you even more absorbed in the moment.

"Being in the now" has been a catch phrase used to describe the importance of the present moment. What time of your life do you have the most control? We know the past is long gone, we have no control. The future is controlled only by the direct action of the present; we have no control there, either. The present moment is the only time that is under your complete control. You can control what you focus on, how you react to what is happening, and what actions you take. If your focus is on past shots or future holes you lose control of you present moment. The goal is to be totally absorbed in what needs to happen now. The practice of meditation is a useful tool to help you stay connected to the present. Meditate by looking at a golf ball and feeling its size, or look at the dimples, and feel the weight. You are bringing your senses together to experience the now. When people first do this exercise they may find themselves mentally drifting away and thinking of something in the past or future. The skill is to bring attention back to the present. No matter how many times you are distracted, bring attention back to the present. The more you practice the easier accomplishing this when you are on the golf course.

Playing with better players can increase your focus for the better or cause your focus to become distracted. Intimidation is something that happens even with the best. When Tiger Woods was winning so many tournaments in 2000-2002 the consensus was that most of the other players were intimidated by Tiger when they saw his name creeping up the leader board. Another players' game is out of your control. What is under your control is how you react to playing with better players. I initially was intimidated by playing with better players, but then I relished the idea of beating them. I might have believed they were better, yet it was fun trying to upset the favorite. Playing as an underdog can be a freeing feeling because the expectations are low and you can play to win.

The ability to focus is the number one skill all champion golfers possess. We are bombarded by numerous potential distractions. Those who can break through the interference will perform the best in the moment. When you are focused on the correct target, our body will execute to that target.

YOUR SHOT

- Practice your 4 focus channel routine

- What part of the focus channel is your strength? Your weakness?

- Identify what pressures get in the way of committing to a shot

- Play to win

- Visualize your shots before you hit them

8

EVALUATE

*The better I have become, the more I have embarrassed myself
by my failures; and the more I have embarrassed myself,
the more I have been goaded into trying to develop greater skills.*
JACK NICKLAUS

chapter

(8)

To improve performance in the future you need to evaluate past performances. Many golfers have a difficult time honestly evaluating their performance. There are two groups of people who don't evaluate: those who think they know it all and those that can't take constructive feedback. However, there are a minority of golfers that take the time to evaluate their performances and find the ways to improve for the next round.

Ways to evaluate:

- Feedback from coach or trusted friend

- Journalize your practice sessions

- Statistics from round of golf

Many golfers blame the wrong areas of their game that often lead to poor performance. Most golfers practice their strengths and are not honest about what they should work on. The best believe they are only as good as the weakest part of their game. Overall improvement should always be the goal. A complete player is hard to come by. However if each part of your game improved by 1% each week you would be a completely different player in a year. Consistent improvement will happen when you become aware of the performance factors of your game.

You should evaluate:

- Your round

- Your practice sessions

- Goal attainment

- Physical conditioning

- Mental skills

Learn from your losses: When we lose an important golf match or tournament we are disappointed. But now what? It is what you do after the round that separates a champion from just an average player. Here are some keys to remember after a tough round.

- Be like a professional- know that a loss can point out strengths and weaknesses, flaws in mental preparation and what should be worked on for the next round

- Don't go in to a round hoping to play well; expect to play well

- Have faith in your athletic ability: you have had success in the past and you will have success in the future

- Ultimately you are competing against yourself, so improve for yourself, not just to win a tournament

Evaluation can come from others or from you. The problem is who you listen to when it comes to taking advice. Most golfers have "rabbit ears"; they will listen to any one who has something to say. These same players are trying out the latest tips in the monthly golf magazine. The best situation is having an instructor you can go to consistently who will give you honest feedback. The longer the student/teacher relationship the easier it is to quickly identify performance gaps. I know that I have had students come to a lesson to "fix" their swing and we spent the time evaluating their entire game. They left with a better plan and used my professional feedback to keep them on track.

If it is in your budget, the best way to get feedback from your instructor is having a playing lesson. I have given numerous playing lessons and learned a lot more about a player in 9 holes than the 10 previous lessons combined. The instructor will provide experience to help you make better decisions, play to your strengths, and see which shots create problems. After the round the instructor will be able to use future lessons more effectively.

If you don't see an instructor regularly the next best way to get feedback is from a regular playing partner. The better the player the better they will be able to pick up on the nuances of the game. The feedback you are looking for includes mechanical issues, course strategy, and mental focus. Someone who plays with you will be able to assist you in giving you feedback.

A useful way to evaluate is through journalizing and data collection. When playing it is a good idea to write down basic stats such as fairways hit, greens in regulation, and putts. After the round compile the statistics in a folder to track your performance. The difficulty of the course should be taken in consideration. Write down the par of the course, the slope rating, and your total score. Now breakdown the round into statistical categories that will serve you based on your performance goals you set earlier in the book. After putting down the statistics write a few sentences on what you did well and what still needs some work. I still have my journals from college that I can reference to learn from what I did well and how I accomplished it. It may be a swing drill that made a big difference or a way I played a particular hole. Take the time to learn from your round.

The same goes for your practice habits. Journalize how much time you are spending in each area of your game. When was the last time you worked on your bunker shots or your 50 yard wedge? Your practice needs to be balanced. So many golfers spend 90% of their time on full swing and forget to practice golf shots. Use some of your practice time to develop better mechanics, however make sure you are spending time on learning golf shots. There is a big difference between practicing your "weight shift" and practicing hitting a pitch shot over a bunker. Balance your time between the training mindset and the trusting mindset. Take time to work on your pre-shot routine, by getting comfortable with making a decision, staying focused, and committing to the shot. Journalize your results after a practice session to remind yourself of what worked and what didn't.

Take responsibility for your results. Champions accept the results of any shot, no matter how bad, and move on to the next shot. A lot of golfers blame the results on everything but themselves. They never learn and stay at that level. We have all played with the golfer who blames every bad shot on a bad bounce or distraction. They continue to complain and the other players get tired of all the excuses for poor play. Don't be one of those players: take responsibility for your results.

The use of a post shot routine is an important element that not many instructors teach. We know about a pre-shot routine; however a lot can be learned from a post shot routine. A post-shot routine is done after a shot is gone. You evaluate what happened with the shot and learn from it. A post-shot routine can keep you mentally and emotionally focused even when the shot is poor.

The post-shot routine can:

- Reinforce great shots you just played. Get exited and remember that feeling.

- Learn from a poor result. Play the shot back as if you did it correctly.

- Analyze by asking, if I had a second chance what would I have done differently mentally or emotionally?

- Move on to the next shot in an emotionally confident state.

The best time to take advantage of proper evaluation is right after a round. Go from the 18th green to the practice tee and your experience will be fresh in your mind. Reinforce the good and work on the few shots you wish you could have played better. This is where you can turn a negative into a positive. So many times when I was playing competitive golf I would leave the course immediately after a bad round. I would take that frustration and disappointment with me home and it affected my mood for the entire evening and sometimes into the next day. I had to learn to evaluate a round immediately afterwards on the practice range and green. My goal of this post round practice was simple; figure out what caused the poor shots. I found that sometimes all it took was 10 minutes of hitting shots to figure out what happened. I also began to evaluate shots based on skill mechanics and mental skill mechanics. This taught me that not all poor shots are because of a physical mechanical breakdown. I found that I may have had a focus problem or my temper affected execution of certain shots. I later went home and replayed these mental breakdowns with how I should have handled the shot. This post round practice helped me regroup and leave the course in a positive mindset. If you don't have time to do physical practice after a round, at least go over the round in your mind later that evening.

YOUR SHOT

- Evaluate your next round and see what really needs improvement

- Remind yourself of what is good about your game

- Look for ways to get the most out of your practice

chapter

PUTTING IT ALL TOGETHER

WHAT YOU WILL LEARN:

- Develop A Plan For Mental Game Improvement

- Commit To Thinking Better On The Course

- Utilize The Many Tools To Play Better

- Enjoy The Journey!

Keep your sense of humor. There's enough stress in the rest of your life to let bad shots ruin a game you're supposed to enjoy.
AMY ALCOTT

The real way to enjoy playing golf is to take pleasure not in the score, but in the execution of the strokes.
BOBBY JONES

chapter

9

This book has provided you with many tools to learn to make you a better golfer. Now is the time to implement these tools so you will improve the skills necessary to be the best you can be. In order to do this you must apply the tools on a consistent basis to truly master them. The first step is to commit to use these new tools.

Let's summarize some of the tools and techniques of this book:

- Goal Setting

- Belief Changing

- Reframing Language

- Visualization

- Anchoring- Optimal Performance State

- Modeling the best

- Focus channels

- Pre-shot routine

- Post shot routine

After a lesson many students feel overwhelmed with all the information that has been told to them. They are confused and don't know what to do first. After reading this book you may have felt the same way. You want to get better, yet you really are not sure how to get started. The best time to start any improvement plan is now.

The first step is for you to go back and review the chapters and answer the questions at the end of the chapters called Your Shot. This helps you prioritize which area you need to spend the most time implementing particular skills. After you have assessed where you are at as it pertains to motivation, goal setting, beliefs, emotional control, focus, execution, and evaluation, rank these in order of weak to strong. Start with your first weakness and go back to that chapter and reread how to improve that area. Commit to working on one area at a time and begin to practice that skill until you have improved. Move on to the next area. What you will find is that improvement in one area will translate to improvement in many areas of the mental game.

Include time in your normal practice sessions to practice the mental skills. If you are hitting balls on the practice range make sure you spend time going through your routine. By being very conscious of learning the routine you could be in essence using several of the mental skills that are needed to play great golf. Your routine consists of having a goal (target), believing you can hit the target, staying focused on the process, being in the optimal arousal state, execution, and evaluation of the shot. If that was the only mental game practice you did you would improve dramatically. The key part of practice is attention and repetition. So many golfers "go through the motions" and hit shots and they may even go through a few shots with their routines. However the level of attention to fully commit to the parts of the routine separates the best from the rest. Remember that Jack Nicklaus has never hit a shot whether in practice or while playing that he first did not visualize beforehand. Are you practicing with that level of discipline? Discipline yourself to repeat these skills with full attention. The more you repeat the faster you will master these skills.

The next step of skill development is to take it on the golf course. If you have worked on a new routine on the practice range and have improved your performance there, it is time to put it to the test. Take the routine out while playing. A new skill does require some conscious thought before it becomes a habit, so stick with it while playing so you can get to the point of owning the skill. There will come a time when you are playing and realize that you hit a shot well without having to think about the mechanics of the routine. Just like making a grip change the golfer that can play through the uncomfortable feelings will ultimately be better in the end.

What is unique about the mental game is that you can practice it almost any where. You can visualize your swing at home before you go to bed. Practicing visualization takes a couple of minutes and can help you with skill development, boost your motivation, or create a game plan for your round. Writing your goals down on a monthly basis takes a few minutes, yet will serve you with motivation to push you toward accomplishment. Get creative in how you go about improving your mental game. For instance I encourage my students to apply these golf mental techniques to the rest of their lives. This could mean being aware of your self talk at all times and creating empowering beliefs for all of parts of your life.

Periodization is a word that is popular in the athletic training community. It is based on the idea of switching your training depending on your goals. The theory is that you want to peak for certain events during the year, so the training needs to be adjusted to reflect those times. In golf you may have an important part of the year where you compete in club or local tournaments and you want to be at your best. Your periodization plan might include heavy physical training in the off season to gain strength and improve flexibility. As you get closer to the time for competition you would back off on the duration and intensity of the physical training. You want to conserve your energy for competition. The off season is a good time to work on improving your golf skills. This may mean practicing more mechanical parts of the game while playing a lot less. The goal is to make the changes well in advance of competition so you can just play. A common mistake golfers make is by changing swings right before an important event. This causes doubt and keeps the golfer in the training mindset on the course. Practice before important events by stressing fundamentals and developing feel for your swing. Another must before an event is to put more focus on your short game. Having a sharp short game will help you tremendously in competition because most golfers don't hit as well in competition as they do in practice. Knowing your short game is solid will take pressure off your full swing.

Your training should include instruction from a professional. Whether it is for your mental game or swing mechanics finding a quality instructor is very important in reaching your golf goals. Since I am a PGA golf professional I have been around those who can teach and those who can't teach. Here are some things to look for in an instructor:

- Personality- You want to be with a positive, energetic individual.

- Experience- Ask for the individual's credentials and teaching experience. Since golf is becoming so specialized I usually recommend working with a full-time instructor. If you take a lesson from a Head Professional at a golf course he or she may only teach 5 to 10 hours per week because they will have many other responsibilities at a course.

- Completeness- An instructor must be open to the idea of complete training. Some instructors are stuck in the Stone Age and don't believe in the importance of physical training or mental training. They say just take lessons and practice more. These instructors are not open to other possibilities for what can help a golfer. Stay away from these types.

- Goal Oriented- Work with instructors who ask you about your goals. These instructors want to see you succeed and will support you during the process.

- Avoid the "quick fix"- Commit to the long-term improvement with an instructor. Don't jump around to many different instructors trying to get the "quick fix".

- Inquire: Ask other good players who they see. I say good players because good players require better instructors. If you want to get better find out who gets good results.

As a student you want to communicate your concerns about your game. Tell your instructor what you have worked on with past instructors. Know your game and tell the instructor what your normal ball flights are, especially under pressure. After a lesson be clear on what are the few keys that you need to work on in the coming weeks. Know what drills you need to do. Also be clear on what the next steps are for future lessons; how are the parts going to make a whole. Be realistic with how long a change will take to become comfortable. Keep focused on the priorities from the lesson; do not stray from the plan.

We all learn in different ways. Great golfers have come from all walks of life with many different methods. In our technologically driven age we have access to some unbelievable equipment. We have computer/video analysis, biomechanical measuring devices, balancing devices; the list grows every year.

As golfers we are searching for the secret and these tools can help us become better golfers if used correctly. But when a golfer relies on technology too much they began to disconnect from the feeling of the game. Golf is a mixture of how we use our eyes, what we feel in our body, and what our mind allows us to perform. My advice is if you take lessons from an instructor who simply relies on video to assess your game then you will have problems. Golf is not about perfect positions; it is about getting the ball in the hole in as few strokes as possible. The ways we learn new movements can be first done statically, then in slow motion, medium speed, and finally full speed. Learning new swing mechanics is the same as learning new mental skills. Take your time understanding the skill, implement the skill in a safe environment, and repeat the skill until you don't have to think about it.

The mental game is sometimes difficult to quantify. The scorecard is used as one of the indicators; however score is not the only way to measure your mental game improvement. The other aspect that gets lost in the pursuit of achievement is enjoyment. After working with thousands of golfers I know that if you are enjoying golf then your mental game is the main reason why. If you can score higher for a particular round and still enjoy the round then you have mastered important mental and emotional skills. We can't control everything on the course. We can control what we think about and how we react to what happens on the golf course.

Golf is a game to be enjoyed. The lure of the game and its challenges can make enjoyment difficult at times. One needs to see the humor in the game to appreciate the ups and downs of what seems a rather simple game. Think back to the last time you laughed on the course. For me it now happens a lot more than it used to. The most important skill set of them all is enjoyment. When you enjoy what you are doing, you will perform better. My fondest memories on the golf course are not of me making a birdie or winning a tournament; it was the unexpected occurrences on the course that made me laugh. From the time a playing partner played a practical joke on another player with an exploding golf ball to the banter between friends, golf is a great experience.

I have been so fortunate to have helped so many golfers that I get to share their enjoyable experiences by listening to their latest game. So many of my students would come to me after a disappointing game and still have smiles on their faces. Their perspective was healthy, they realized they didn't have to play golf, they chose to play golf. You choose to tee it up to play; you also choose the level of enjoyment you will experience.

My favorite story that illustrates the humor of golf came from one of my students. He is a very good player who is pursuing the goal of getting to the PGA Tour. He had an important tournament that he had been preparing for that potentially could provide him with an opportunity to make a significant amount of money and build his confidence for tournaments later in the season. He ended up playing poorly the first round and basically had no chance to win. His wife and friends were scheduled to drive down and see him play on the weekend provided he made the cut. His wife calls him after the poor first round and asks what he has to shoot to make the cut. The player's response, "I have to shoot about half the field". This player could still see humor in what was a disappointing time for him. By seeing the humor we can bounce back from poor performances and be ready for the next round.

I could fill a book with all the funny experiences that I have had and those that I have heard. Take time to reconnect with all the great experiences that you have had on the golf course. You can use these positive memories to boost your mood when you are down and motivate you to look at golf for what it is, a great game.

YOUR SHOT

- Reconnect with your goals on a weekly basis

- Schedule your practice time

- Prioritize to improve your weaknesses

- Train all parts or your game- Mechanical, physical, and mental

- Change the way you think!

- What is the first mental skill that you will practice?

- How are you going to implement this skill into your practice?

- When was a time you had the most fun on the golf course?

- How can you enjoy golf more?

LEARNING FROM THE LINKS

WHAT YOU WILL LEARN:

- How To Apply The Mental Game Skills To Improve Your Life

- How To Apply These Principles In The Business Arena

Golf is the "only-est" sport.
You're completely alone with every conceivable opportunity to defeat yourself.
Golf brings out your assets and liabilities as a person. The longer you play,
the more certain you are that a man's performance is the
outward manifestation of who, in his heart, he really thinks he is.
HALE IRWIN

You are what you think you are- in golf and in life.
RAYMOND FLOYD

To find a man's true character, play golf with him.
P.G. WODEHOUSE-WRITER

c h a p t e r

(10)

There is no royal road to success. The path is not an easy one, which is one of the chief reasons why golf has such an enduring lure.
WALTER J. TRAVIS

If you can't enjoy the time between the golf shots, then you are going to have a pretty difficult life because most of your life is the time spent in-between.
PETER JACOBSEN

What golf has taught me is more than how to play a game. Golf has provided a way for me to challenge myself. I have learned how to deal with failure, discipline myself to reach a goal, and play by the rules. Sounds a little bit like life doesn't it? In this chapter I will cover how to take the lessons of golf to improve your life.

When you have played golf for any length of time you begin to appreciate all the lessons that the game teaches. This book has been about how to improve your golf performance by applying the mental and emotional skills that champion golfers possess. Golf is a journey with many unexpected destinations. Some of the stops are painful: like the times you played poorly at a tournament. Some of the stops are joyful; like the time you beat your golf buddies for the first time. Golf is a sport that you can control only so much. The way the ball bounces, your competitor, and the environment are all out of your control. How you deal with the uncontrollable is more about you as a person than you as a golfer.

To succeed in the life is very much the same journey. We all aspire to have great lives. We dream of how things should be and we make plans to bring ourselves closer to that dream. Along the way the road takes many twists and turns. Just as we want to enjoy and succeed in golf through practice and playing, life requires us, on a daily basis, to show up as a champion athlete. The pressures we feel on the golf course are no match for the pressures that we feel in our lives. However, the skills that are in this book can be applied to your life to bring more fulfillment, more joy, and help you achieve your goals.

A group of individuals who have taught me more about golf and dealing with performance were the golfers of the Tri-Valley Special Olympics golf team. I have been the head coach for the past ten years and marvel at the way these athletes perform. They have positive attitudes and are always trying their best on every shot. They rarely think about the outcome of their score. Their only goal is to enjoy each moment of playing. The joy they get from making a one foot putt is more than most players get from making a birdie. They are respectful of their playing partners, support others when they are down, and can't wait until the next time they get to play golf. Just thinking of how they play changes my perspective on golf and life.

What can we learn from golf? Golf teaches us patience, focus, dealing with failures, dealing with obstacles, getting along with others, pulling off the impossible, risking, and discipline. The best demonstrate these characteristics under competitive pressure. What have you learned from golf? How has playing golf made you a better person?

APPLYING THESE PRINCIPLES TO YOUR BUSINESS

What has been an unexpected turn in my career is the application of these performance principles to the business sector. After sharing these mental game principles with my students they all tell me how these principles have improved their business performance. Now I have been asked to share these powerful techniques to sales staffs, executives, and leaders of teams who are looking for proven ways to optimize performance.

Business is a competition and the winner will be the one who can stay motivated, focus on the most important elements, and execute despite distractions. If you have already achieved success as a business person, look at what made that happen. Apply those skills to your golf game. It works both ways. Performance on the golf course is the same in the boardroom as it is in your life.

Would you do business with someone who cheated on the course or couldn't control his emotions? Probably not, so you have to be in control of how you perform on the course. A lot of business is done on the golf course and how you carry yourself as a person is a lot more important than final score. As you improve your mental and emotional skills for golf, you can improve your performance skills in business.

In golf and business we must first master the fundamentals before we achieve greatness. The challenges that golf provides are the same as with business. Both require desire, dedication, focus, and mental toughness. A top CEO always goes back to fundamentals to solve problems and pushes his team to the next level.

Taking the lessons we have learned from golf to our life is a game in and of itself. Every day is like a new round. We have a target for how we want the day to go, however there are distractions and obstacles in the way. How do you handle the interference? Do you continue to focus on the target or do you get frustrated with the stresses of life? Each moment of your life is like another shot. You can stay completely attentive to the present and get the most out of it. Unfortunately many live life like playing golf. They are scared of the hazards and never commit to letting go. The zone in golf is achieved through preparation, focus, and letting go. Living life by these steps would bring more joy with less stress.

Being your best emotionally on and off the golf course would serve you no matter the situation. Dealing with the bad bounces of a golf ball or the disappointment of a lost job shows the character of you as an individual. Taking responsibility for our actions is ultimately the most empowering trait you can possess. In golf it is just you and the ball. The ball just goes where your actions take it. In life it is the same way; you will go where your actions take you. Each shot is a new chance of where you want the ball to go. Each day is a new chance of where you want your life to go. Each shot and each day allow you to react emotionally any way that you choose.

It is all about performance. How are you going to perform today? Will it be with frustration and stress or with focus and confidence? Take these performance skills to every part of your life to achieve your goals and enjoy the process.

Thank you for taking your valuable time to take your golf game to the next level by utilizing the mental and emotional skills of the best. As your goals change revisit this book to take yourself to the next level. This is a fun journey and we are lucky to play the great game of golf.

Golf is life. We only get out of it what we put into it. When we have the desire to be better, believe we can do it, focus on what is important, execute despite the fears, and learn from our results we guarantee that our golf and our life are both filled with success and joy.

YOUR SHOT

- Start today and go for your goals

- Apply these techniques to all areas of your life

- Everyday is a new round- stay focused and confident

- Enjoy the Journey!

Rick Sessinghaus specializes in increasing people's performance in their personal, business and athletic careers through speaking, training, and coaching. Rick founded Sessinghaus Performance Systems with the purpose of helping others realize their full potential and live their dreams. Rick got his start helping athletes, chiefly golfers, improve their competitiveness. When Rick was presented with the opportunity to use these performance principles in other fields he soon discovered a demand for his coaching method for clients' personal and professional lives. He helped them find success equal to that of his athletic clients.

Now Rick Sessinghaus offers the same proven success formula that has helped athletes to anyone motivated to live like a champion. Rick has now found more satisfaction helping others achieve their dreams than he did in his own competitive career, and he has devoted his life to the study of peak performance. Long intrigued by the fact that physical skills were rarely the determining factor in athletic success, Rick studied the mental and emotional skills that make or break a performance. Adding to his Bachelors Degree in Speech Communications, Rick received his Doctorate Degree in Applied Sports Psychology.

Synthesizing the tools and methods of Olympic champions, top business executives, and others who have achieved a life of greatness, Rick developed a proven system that can raise an individual or team's level of performance regardless of where they are beginning. He specializes in assessing how an individual can best integrate his or her mind, body, and skills to reach his or her full potential. As Rick continues to enrich the quality of people's lives through his proven performance enhancement system, he is constantly researching the latest scientific finding pertinent to achievement. Rick lives with his beautiful wife Kathy and daughters Grace and Katy, and son Grant in Burbank, CA.

To find out more about how Rick Sessinghaus can help your performance visit www.RickSessinghaus.com.

references

Adler, H. & Morris, K. 1997. *Masterstroke: Use The Power Of Your Mind To Improve Your Golf With NLP*. London: Piatkus.

Bonk, T. 2006, August 25. "Mental Plan." *Los Angeles Times*. pp. D1, D9.

Clark, B. 2004. "Expert Golf Instructors' Student-teacher Interaction Patterns." *Research Quarterly for Exercise and Sport*. Retrieved March 24, 2006, from HighBeam Research.

Cochran, A. 1994. *Golf the Scientific Way*, Hemel Hempstead Hertfordshire, U.K.: Aston Publishing Group.

Cochran, A.J. & Farrally M.R. 1999. *Science and Golf III*. Champaign, IL: Human Kinetics.

Cohn, P. 2000. *Peak Performance Golf*, Chicago, IL: Contemporary Books.

Cohn, P. & Winters, R. 1995. *The Mental Art of Putting: Using your Mind to Putt Your Best*. South Bend, IN: Diamond Communications.

Coop, R. 1993. *Mind Over Golf*. Macmillian.

MacRury, D. 1997. *Golfers on Golf*. Los Angeles: General Publishing Group.

Marriott, L. & Nilsson, P. 2005. *Every Shot Must Have a Purpose*. New York: Gotham Books.

Nideffer, R. 1992. *Psyched To Win*. Champaign, IL: Human Kinetics.

Orlick, T. 1990. *In Pursuit of Excellence* 2nd ed.. Champaign, IL: Human Kinetics.

Orlick, T. 1986. *Psyching for Sport: Mental Training for Athletes*. Champaign, IL: Human Kinetics.

Parent, J. 2002. *Zen Golf*. New York: Doubleday.

Shaw, D.F. 2002. "The Effects Of Outcome Imagery On Golf-putting Performance." *Journal of Sports Sciences*. Retrieved March 24, 2006, from HighBeam Research.

Toole, T. 1999. "The Learning Advantages Of An External Focus Of Attention In Golf." *Research Quarterly for Exercise and Sport*. Retrieved March 23, 2006, from HighBeam Research.

Woodman, T. 2005. "Conscious Processing, Stress And Focus Of Attention In Skilled Golfer." *Journal of Sports Sciences*. Retrieved March 23, 2006, from HighBeam Research.

CPSIA information can be obtained at www.ICGtesting.com
Printed in the USA
268588BV00001B/20/A